MAX IN VERSE

Max in Verse

Rhymes and Parodies by
MAX BEERBOHM

Collected and Annotated by
J. G. RIEWALD

HEINEMANN: LONDON

William Heinemann Ltd

LONDON MELBOURNE TORONTO

CAPE TOWN AUCKLAND

First published in Great Britain 1964

© 1963 by J. G. Riewald

PRINTED IN GREAT BRITAIN BY OFFSET LITHOGRAPHY BY
BILLING AND SONS LTD., GUILDFORD AND LONDON

Permission to reprint extracts from the previously unpublished work of Max Beerbohm, and from his published works, is given by the Administratrix of the Estate of Sir Max Beerbohm and by William Heinemann Limited. For permission to use other copyright material, the Editor is grateful to the following publishers, editors and representatives: the Editor of *The Abinger Chronicle*, Abinger Common, Surrey, for 'Old Surrey Saws and Sayings'; The British Broadcasting Corporation for 'In Max's top hat'; Marguerite Steen for the commentary on Beerbohm's 'Lines to be Hung in a Hotel Bedroom at Charing Cross' from *William Nicholson* by Marguerite Steen; the Representatives of John Drinkwater and Sidgwick and Jackson Ltd, for 'Cottage Song' from *The Collected Poems of John Drinkwater;* Gerald Duckworth and Co. Ltd for a Beerbohm verse from *Celebrities and Simple Souls* by Alfred Sutro; the Editor of the *Evening Citizen*, Glasgow, for a limerick ascribed to Max Beerbohm; Faber and Faber Ltd, for Beerbohm verses from *Men and Memories, 1900-1922* and *Since Fifty: Men and Memories, 1922-1938* by William Rothenstein; William Heinemann Ltd for the explanation of the sonnet 'To Henry James' from *The Life and Letters of Sir Edmund Gosse* by Evan Charteris, and for 'The Prayer' from *The Collected Poems of John Galsworthy*; Putnam and Co. Ltd for a Beerbohm verse from *The Romantic '90s* by Richard Le Gallienne; Sotheby and Co. for the verse of Max Beerbohm illustrated in their catalogue of his library and literary manuscripts, and for the jacket self-caricature from the same source.

TO

LORD DAVID CECIL

CONTENTS

ACKNOWLEDGMENTS

My special thanks are due to the Administratrix of the Estate of the late Sir Max Beerbohm for permission to print his poems and to quote from his writings. For permission to reproduce manuscript material and for many other kindnesses I am most grateful to Dr. Roger Highfield, Librarian of Merton College, Oxford; W. H. Bond, Curator of Manuscripts, The Houghton Library, Harvard University; Professor William A. Jackson, Harvard University; Lord David Cecil, New College, Oxford; the Manuscript Department of the British Museum; E. E. Bissell, Ashorne, Warwick; Joseph Bransten, San Francisco; William W. Clary, Los Angeles, and Dr. Davies, Librarian of the Honnold Library of The Claremont Colleges, Claremont, California; C. F. H. Evans, Librarian of Charterhouse, Godalming, Surrey; Professor Majel Ewing, Los Angeles; Professor G. Giovannini, Washington, D. C.; Miss Diana Gould, Smith College, Northampton, Massachusetts; Professor Robert Graves, Deyá, Mallorca, Spain; Stephen and Janet Greene, Dover, Vermont; Jay Hall, Statesville, North Carolina; Rupert Hart-Davis, London; Sir Geoffrey Keynes, Brinkley, Newmarket, Suffolk; David Magee, San Francisco; William A. von Metz, Oakland, California; Simon Nowell-Smith, President of the Bibliographical Society, Oxford; David Posner, Lockwood Memorial Library, University of Buffalo, Buffalo, New York; Sir John Rothenstein, Director of the Tate Gallery, Newington, Warborough, Oxford; and Mrs. Sylvia Sprigge, Abinger Common, Surrey.

I should also like to thank the following individuals for their help in tracking down the manuscripts: S. N. Behrman, New York City; Trevor J. Brown, of B. F. Stevens and Brown Ltd, London; Alexander P. Clark, Curator of Manuscripts, Princeton University Library; Leon Drucker, London; Ifan Kyrle Fletcher, London; Mrs. Nellie Guedalla, London; James J. Heslin, Director of the New-York Historical Society, New York; Robert W. Hill, Keeper of Manuscripts, The New York Public Library, New York; P. Leigh-Smith, St. Tropez,

Var, France; David I. Masson, The Brotherton Library, University of Leeds, Leeds; Percy H. Muir, Takeley, Bishops Stortford; Professor David A. Randall, Librarian of The Lily Library, Indiana University, Bloomington, Indiana; Sir Sydney C. Roberts, Cambridge; Ian Robertson, of the Ashmolean Museum, Oxford; Anthony B. Rota, of Bertram Rota Ltd, London; A. K. Russell, of Francis Edwards Ltd, London; the Director of the Seven Gables Bookshop, New York; G. F. Sims, Hurst, Reading, Berkshire; Oliver Stallybrass, Deputy Librarian of the London Library, London; Professor Stanley Weintraub, Pennsylvania State University, University Park, Pennsylvania; Brooke Whiting, of the Department of Special Collections of the Library of the University of California, Los Angeles; and Miss Marjorie G. Wynne, Librarian, Rare Book Room, Yale University Library.

J. G. R.

PREFACE

MAX BEERBOHM: CARICATURIST AND WRITER, 1872-1956. These words are inscribed on the stone plaque above Sir Max Beerbohm's grave in the crypt of St. Paul's Cathedral, London, and though one might quarrel about the order of the epithets, it is as a caricaturist and a writer of brilliantly amusing prose that he is known to the world.

But Max in *verse*? Despite William Empson who, in *Seven Types of Ambiguity,* included him among the poets on the strength of a passage from *Zuleika Dobson,* Beerbohm is not generally thought of as a writer of verse. His name does not occur in the anthologies of English poetry, nor is it found in the current collections of humorous poems. Of course many people know his " 'Savonarola' Brown," the most effective parody of pseudo-Shakespearean verse-drama ever written, and his equally effective "Sequelula" to Hardy's *The Dynasts,* but they often do not know that there is so much more. Humbert Wolfe, in his *Notes on English Verse Satire,* somewhat mistakenly regretted the fact that this ambidextrous artist had not thought fit to clinch his triumph by making a more frequent use of the vehicle of verse, and even distinguished Beerbohm collectors do not always realize that, in addition to these large verse parodies, Sir Max had written a considerable number of shorter rhymes, both in English and in Latin. Besides being a source of delight, some of these poetical performances might help us to get a deeper insight into that most inscrutable of characters: "Max."

So when, in the autumn of 1961, my friend Stephen Greene, book publisher and long-time collector of Maxiana, during one of his visits to Europe asked me about the feasibility of editing another volume of Beerbohm's unpublished writings, I boldly suggested that a slim volume of his *œuvres poétiques* would not be inopportune, remembering what Sir Max once wrote me: "I have written so little that I don't want less than that to be available." But my initial enthusiasm was somewhat damped when I found that my labor in tracking down Beerbohm's poems, which had been scattered in the *diaspora* of the Sotheby sale of his library and literary manuscripts in 1960, would be more herculean than that of John Lane when he compiled the first Beerbohm bibliography in 1896. However, thanks to the generous aid of numerous private collectors, antiquarian booksellers and institutional libraries on both sides of the Atlantic, it has been possible to make accessible to a wider circle of connoisseurs most of the verse known to have been written by Max Beerbohm.

A few of the poems here collected occur in his own volumes; some were brought to light from such "inilluminable catacombs" as *The Winter Owl* (—no copy in the British Museum or in the London Library), or published from privately printed and strictly limited editions; a large number of them have never appeared in print before.

In an undertaking of this kind certain desiderata will always remain. Thus one would have liked to include Beerbohm's alternative ending to Yeats's "Ballad of the Foxhunter," beginning with those classical lines:

> Hark forard, away, and down with Yeats!
> Begorra, he droives me mad.

But unfortunately, this piece and certain others, of whose existence I am aware, have continued to elude my patient researches. On the other hand I have included a few *bouts-rimés* that are not wholly Beerbohm's. They are the product of the sonnet game which he used to play with his friends, and which he himself had invented. By the terms of this game each player alternately contributed a line to the poem until it was finished. Of these compositions, which are sometimes slightly malicious, or scatological, or of the kind known as "curious," only a few specimens survive.

And then, of course, there are what Humbert Wolfe once described as "certain privately circulated excursions which Charles II would have welcomed, but which are not believed to be safe for democracy." This was written in 1929, and apparently refers to such pungent plays-of-wit as the "Ballade Tragique à Double Refrain," which is said to have delayed Beerbohm's knighthood for twenty years. That it was never Max's aim to attack or undermine Royalty is abundantly clear from his works. In his essay on George IV, written in 1894, he had playfully raised the question "whether Royalty, as a wholly Pagan institution, is not out of place in a community of Christians." In "Some Words on Royalty," originally written in 1898, he had ironically suggested wax robots as a means of escaping the moral responsibility of ruining a whole family. Ten years later his attitude had boiled down to the commonsensical "Human nature being what it is, a monarchy is the best expedient, all the world over" ("Porro Unum . . ."); and by 1926, in the days of the general strike in England, his feelings towards Royalty had definitively evolved from the satirically-indifferent to the seriously-appreciative. It is this same spirit which informs the following passage from a letter which he wrote to me from Rapallo after the catastrophic inundations of Holland and England early in 1953: "Miss Jungmann and I heard on the 'wireless' the voice of Prince Bernhard, condoling with England before he mentioned Holland. A beautiful voice and manner. We were deeply moved. I am glad there are still royal dynasties here and there."

This volume contains eighty-four poems, of which thirty-four have never been published in any form. Of the remaining fifty, eighteen have appeared in Max Beerbohm's own works, eleven in books by others, ten in auction catalogues, seven in newspapers or in limited-circulation periodicals, and four in small private editions. A few are immature work, written between the ages of seventeen and twenty, whose interest lies in their precocity and in illustrating his development as a writer of light verse. The inclusion of certain other pieces should be judged of in the light of his dictum: "Only mediocrity can be trusted to be always at its best." The poems cover a period of over sixty years, the first dating from 1890, the last from 1952. Since they are so seldom "current-eventful," it was virtually impracticable to print them under headings reflecting the background of national or world events at the time of writing. Rather than force them into more or less arbitrary compartments, I have adopted, as far as possible, a classification according to the places and periods in which they were written. Within these groups the items are arranged in a roughly chronological order, according to the actual or approximate time of composition.

Apart from reasons of space, my justification for detaching *Savonarola* from its prose context may be found in the circumstance that the play belongs to an earlier stage of composition than the narrative frame in which it is embedded. On the other hand things like "Carmen Becceriense," or the deathless lines to Henry James ascribed to Miss Peploe, would have lost too much of their bite if they had been divorced from their setting. Where more than one version exists, I have printed what seemed to me to be the more authentic one. In some of the manuscripts there occur variant readings from which I have been compelled to select. Since this little book does not pretend to be a Critical Edition of The Poetical Works of Sir Max Beerbohm, I have been content to record these cases in the notes at the end of it. Besides stating the source of the rhymes, these notes also give further bibliographical information. In order to add to the reader's immediate enjoyment, many of the poems are preceded by short introductory comments providing the necessary background and explaining certain allusions.

Not long ago it was observed by Professor C. S. Lewis that "to a real lover of literature an exquisitely made *divertissement* is a very much more respectable thing than some of the 'philosophies of life' which are foisted upon the great poets." However this may be, some of the things collected in this book certainly belong to the category of exquisitely made divertissements, and it is my hope that Max in verse will command the respect, and even the admiration, of that same fit-though-few minority upon which the fate of his prose works depends. For, as he once wrote to Sir Sydney Roberts, "it is only the good opinion of the few that keeps a book alive."

University of Groningen,   J. G. RIEWALD
Netherlands
January 1963

Charterhouse and Oxford

1890-1895

§ 1

CARMEN BECCERIENSE

CUM PROLEGOMENIS ET COMMENTARIO CRITICO

EDIDIT H. M. B.

1 Beccerius (dictu miserum) mortalibus ægris
   Concertum quondam Becceriense dabat.

A poem of singular power and beauty, and of the utmost historical value. Its authorship has been and still is disputed; so, in order to set all doubts at rest, I may at once state that I attribute it to the pen of Lucretius. I say this mainly because my old and valued friend Professor Mayor is convinced that it was written by Juvenal.

1. *Beccerius.* Of Beccerius Naso Pianonicus little is known; save from the famous hexameter of Ennius:

   'Ingenui voltus et spectaculatus ocellos.'

   Mortalibus ægris. The same phrase is found several times in Virgil's writings. The words are the eloquent offspring of that spirit of pessimism which also prompts the poet to speak of '*nimio* plausu' (l. 3) and '*notos* ignes' (l. 5).

2. *Concertum.* Late, very late, Latin. Our word 'concert' is said to be derived from the same root, and indeed the etymology seems not unlikely. See also my old friend and schoolfellow Professor Madvig's most learned note on 'Entertainments.'

   Dabat. Fine word; note too the desponding use of the imperfect. A less skilful poet would have said 'dedit,' but not so Lucretius.

Ecce, salutatus nimio plausu puerorum
    Blande subridensque editiora petit.
5 Incipiens, animi notos bene temperat ignes,
    Mox tamen innumeras jactat ubique manus.
Usque graves gravibus superinjicit ictibus ictus,
    Mixtaque cum mixtis sunt nota mixta notis.

3. *Nimio.* We have it on the authority of an early writer that Cornelius Grano was thus applauded for no less than ten minutes. Whether Lucretius was justified in the present instance in calling the applause 'nimius' is not a question of vital import. The true poet is not shackled by petty and trivial details, but my old friend Professor Mayor is.

   Plausu. 'Apud Carthusianos non necessarie signum popularitatis' (The Scholiast).

4. *Blande subridensque.* Notice the overlapping syllable *que*, by which the poet describes the breadth of Beccerius' smile. It is in these little homely but exquisite touches that we recognise the true artist. Needless to say my old friend and schoolfellow Professor Mayor entirely failed to appreciate this exquisite line.

   Editiora. Poet. for the platform.

5. *Notos.* See my excellent note on line 1.

6. *Innumeras* κ.τ.λ. Needless difficulties have been made over this line. Some suggest to take it thus: 'he scatters up and down his unnumbered hands.' But seeing that this theory depends upon the absurd supposition that Beccerius possessed more hands than other people, I dismiss it instantly. By far the simplest and most straightforward way of rendering it is 'he shakes on every side innumerable hands,' i.e. he shakes hands all round. Cf. the custom common among pugilists of shaking hands before an encounter.

7, 8. Perhaps the finest lines in the poem.

   Nota. From *notum*=a note. Look this word out in your Latin-English. Conington, elegantly:—'And mixèd notes with mixèd notes are mixed.'

Nos aures premimus dextris, ridetque Robinso,
10   Musicus instructor nam fuit alter. Hibus
Contremefacta sonis lacrumas Concordia fundit,
Et fugit ex Aula, diva repulsa, Nova.
Sic fugat impietate deam, fugat ipse sacerdos,
Sic caret Harmonia Carthusiana domus.

9. *Nos.* A graphic touch, from which many commentators have assumed
that Lucretius was himself one of the audience; but the dispute
as to whether he occupied a seat in Block E or in Block C can
only be carried on by guesswork.

Ridet. Zumpt idiotically understands 'lætitia' after this word, but
it cannot be that professional jealousy had infected the peaceful
breasts of the twin music masters of the Alma Domus.

Robinso. 'Blandus homo et suavissimus' (Cicero).

10. *Hibus.* Archaic form of abl. pl. of *hic, hæc, hoc.* By such forms the
poet seeks to add an old-world dignity to his subject. My old
friend and schoolfellow, with characteristic impudence, wishes to
substitute the word *hiemps,* thus ruining the whole tone and
grandeur of the verse. See also Mr. T. E. Page, admirably:—'Some
people would like to re-write the classics, please, if they got
the chance.'

By the sudden and unusual transition of sense at the end of the
pentameter the poet evidently suggests something or other; what, we
are not quite sure, but the idea is none the less skilfully suggested.

11. *Contremefacta.* Very strong word, and an ἅπαξ εἰρημένον.

12. *Aula Nova.* A large building of defective acoustic properties.

Fugit. 'She runs away' (Conington). There were four exits by which
Concordia might have made her escape. Personally I incline to believe that she made it by the front door on the left-hand side.
The question is, however, trivial—indeed its very triviality is the
best excuse I can offer for the space I have devoted to its discussion.

13, 14. *Sic—sic.* Emphatic repetition, and highly effective in the peroration
of the poem.

14. *Carthusiana domus.* A fine phrase, found elsewhere. But beware of
regarding it as a tag.

§ 2

Elegiac couplets on Charterhouse

FLORUIT innumeros Schola Carthusiana per annos,
    Olim Londinii pessima pernicies.
FLORET in aerio jam condita vertice montis
    Quingentosque docet tristitiam pueros.
FLOREBIT, nec non Plutonis regna manebunt.
    Altera ut agnoscam sum memor alterius.

§ 3

On W. S. Gilbert

'Horrendum et dictu video mirabile monstrum.'
    Gilbertus culpas sentiit Ipse suas ! ! ! ! !

§ 4

Damnosa Senectus

Infelix, cui sorte datum est, pereuntibus annis,
Munditias sentire suae vanescere formae;
Quaeque tot exhaurit suspiria pectore ab imo
Ut deus injecta caligine damnet ocellos,
Impatiens. Vitae cui lux incertior ardet,
Rugosam frontem cura est ornare capillis
Quot bene servavit, dentato pectine captos.
Quae pede praetereunte reliquit in ore Saturnus,
Tristis anus, quantum possit, vestigia cretis
Hic niveis, illic rubro medicamine supplet.

Nigrantes niveo velantur tegmine crines,
 Recta-que bisectans tendit ubique via.
Jamque genas varii certant vitiare colores,
 Segnis eo gressu difficilique pede.
Jamque, modo celeris, res est raucissima risus;
 Quod nisi per vitrum conspicio nihil est.
Cum tempus nova saecla, novos evolverit annos,
 Heu minor exigua forma superstes erit.

Membra mei, quondam formosa, informia fiunt,
 Formaque, tam tenuis quae fuit ante, fuit.
Forma fuit; quamvis stringunt retinacula firma,
 Improba confines nescit habere suos.
Plus-que gerens oneris quam prima aetate gerebam,
 Crescit adhuc, dempto limite, crescit onus.
Cum tempus nova saecla, novos evolverit annos,
 Ingenti major forma superstes erit.

§ 5. To Reginald Turner, while they were both undergraduates in Oxford.

Rondeau d'Admonition

You silly fool, why *do* you lie
So late abed nor ever try
    To get your breakfast done by ten
    Read through your 'Telegraph' and then
Start working with alacrity.

Now ev'ry morn your sluggish eye
Abhors your books, what time you ply
    Your essays with a faulty pen
        You silly fool !

You never missed your rollers: why
    Remit that virtuous regimen ?
    Late hours were never meant for men. . . .
But there—there—there——you needn't cry
        You silly fool !

§ 6

Ballade de la Vie Joyeuse

Why do men feast upon wormwood and gall
　　When there are roses for every day?
Let us not leave them to fade on the wall,
　　Knowing of naught but 'la vie limitée.'
　　Is there a heaven? Be that as it may
Conduct's an image of priest-eaten wood.
　　We are but bits of elaborate clay.
Let us be happy without being good.

Ah! but the life is not easy to all.
　　Often the enemy drives us to bay
And, as we faint in the Philistine brawl
　　Utilitarians haply will say:
　　'Virtue, my friends, is not much in the way,
Try it: nor think that it possibly could
　　Hinder voluptuous ecstasy.'—Nay
Let us be happy *without* being good.

Many a Hedonist, pressed by the small
　　Moralists out of the ethical fray,
Weary at last of defying Saint Paul
　　Charters Morality's one-horse shay.
　　Even the author of 'Dorian Gray'
Makes for his hero a virtuous mood;

Let us take warning—let *us* not obey
Let us be happy without being good.

L'ENVOI

God, we address you for once and away
Nor do we pester for heavenly food—
This is the gist of our litany:—Pray
Let us be happy without being good.

§ 7

'Doubt Divine'

Do we then live or are we nothingness?
    What are the stars in heaven,
    The earth, or darkness riven,
Life's tiny measures and her weariness?

Best that we know not—(if indeed we know
    Not)—ere the hour be gone
    When round the judgement throne
We stand and cry to Heaven 'Be it so!'

So be it:—if the Magdalen's caress
    Can stay the Martyr's tear,
    What is our substance here?
Do we then live or are we nothingness?

§ 8

In Max's copy of J. K. Stephen's *Lapsus Calami*

'From C. S. C. to J. K. S.
The mantle has descended.'
So through the book, in dull distress,
I wended.——Having wended,
With sweet alacrity I flee
From J. K. S. to C. S. C.

London

1895-1910

§ 9

On the imprint of the first English edition of
The Works of Max Beerbohm

'London: JOHN LANE, *The Bodley Head*
    New York: CHARLES SCRIBNER'S SONS.'
This plain announcement, nicely read,
    Iambically runs.

§ 10

On a performance of
Ali Baba and the Forty Thieves

Full many Panto's truly there have been,
But this the best of all is, I do ween.
Each one is always better than the last,
And Mr. Collins has himself surpass'd
In Ali Baba and the Forty Thieves.
And yet, somehow (to say so me it grieves!)
I can't with truth declare I much enjoyed it—
But don't suppose I mean *you* should avoid it!
The fault's my *own,* and, for that reason very,
I'd best *own* up and bid you all be merry!
If I myself don't like this Pantomime,
Live and let live, boys!—it is all the same!
To Drury Old, I'm certain, when you go, you——

BUT I have written quite enough to show you, reader, how fearfully I have been haunted by the rhyming iambics in 'Ali Baba' at Drury Lane, and in 'Dick Whittington' at the Adelphi. In point of rhythm my lines are perhaps superior to them, but I think I have managed to suggest the kind of order in which the words come tripping, and also the level of humour and sense above which they seldom rise. . . .

§ 11

An appreciation of Professor Mueller

The old man named Mullar
Who read all the works of Max Mueller,
    And asked were they dull,
    Replied 'Very dull,
And they get duller and duller.'

§ 12

In Max's copy of William Rothenstein's *Goya*

I find I can often enjoy a
Half-hour with the glories of Goya.
    At the end of that time
    I acknowledge that I'm
Averse from the glories of Goya.

§ 13

Ballade of 'Another Luminary'

Of the persons whose work will endure
    For ever, as models to those
Who are practising Literature,

Jerome Klapka Jerome, we suppose,
    Is the prime and unparalleled rose,
And scents the tip-toppermost heights;
    But near to that proud flower grows
Mr. Turner, the author of 'Tights.'

Barry Pain's is a pen that is 'pure'
    And 'trembling' wherever it flows;
The 'pars' of Vandam have '*allure*';
    Nathaniel Gubbins one knows;
    Robert Barr is a master-mind; so's
Jimmy Davis. But none of them writes
    Quite like that sweet wielder of Prose,
Mr. Turner, the author of 'Tights.'

Arrive! What cloud shall obscure
    His glory? What Cromwell depose
Him, the kingly and kindly imbuer
    Of all things with beauty? What foes,
    Grown glaucous through envious throes,
Shall maim in his heavenly flights
    Or mar in his earthly repose
Mr. Turner, the author of 'Tights'?

ENVOI

Prince, why should you turn up your nose
At one in whom Greening delights?
Hats off! and look slippy! There goes
Mr. Turner, the author of 'Tights.'

§ 14. To Richard Le Gallienne, who had forsaken England to live in New York.

To Dick

O witched by American bars !
Pan whistles you home on his pipes.
We love you for loving the stars,
But what *can* you see in the stripes ?

§ 15

Autobiography

The one quality that Max
Conspicuously lacks
Is a certain High Seriousness, which may be met
In *The Pall Mall Gazette.*

§ 16

After Kipling's *Barrack-Room Ballads*

Then it's collar 'im tight,
    In the name o' the Lawd !
'Ustle 'im, shake 'im till 'e's sick !
    Wot, 'e *would*, would 'e ? Well,
    Then yer've got ter give 'im 'Ell,
An' it's trunch, trunch, truncheon does the trick.
POLICE STATION DITTIES.

§ 17

Triolets by A. C. B.

You 'ld think I must be a clergyman,
　　So like one do I write.
When I break the news about Queen Anne,
You 'ld think I must be a clergyman.
No dips in my ample tub of bran
　　Bring aught but bran to light:
You 'ld think I *must* be a clergyman,
　　So like one do I write.

And yet I am as lay as you—
　　Ah me, the pity of 't !
My upturn'd eyes are heavenly blue,
And yet I am as lay as you.
Naught that I write is not ter-rew
　　And trite and sweet and soft,
And yet I am as lay as you—
　　Ah me, the pity of 't !

　　　I wish I had been Papa,
　　　　That arresting Archbishop.
　　Crozier'd Cantuar !—
　　I wish I had been Papa.
　　Whenever folk murmur 'Bah !
　　　　What sermons you dish up,'
　　I wish I had been Papa,
　　　　That arresting Archbishop.

Nevertheless, it is my bounden duty to drone on;
    And, even were it not, on I should drone.
'Tis hard to keep an always Christian tone in Babylon;
Nevertheless, it is my bounden duty to drone on.

The Eighteenth-Century divines' tone in comparison
    With mine was an inebriating tone . . .
Nevertheless, it is my bounden duty to drone on;
    And, even were it not, on I should drone.

§ 18

Chorus of a song that might have been written by Albert Chevalier

I drops in to see young Ben
In 'is tap-room now an' then,
And I likes to see 'im gettin' on becoz
    'E's got pluck and 'e's got brains,
    And 'e takes no end o' pains,
But——'e'll never be the man 'is Father woz.

§ 19. The earliest known example of Max's delight in his sonnet game, in which he and a friend—in this case Edmund Gosse—wrote alternate lines on an agreed-upon theme. The odd-numbered lines are Max's.

To Henry James

Say, indefatigable alchemist,
Melts not the very moral of your scene,
Curls it not off in vapour from between
Those lips that labour with conspicuous twist?
Your fine eyes, blurred like arc-lamps in a mist,
Immensely glare, yet glimmerings intervene,
So that your May-Be and your Might-Have-Been
Leave us still plunging for your genuine gist.
How different from Sir Arthur Conan Doyle,—
As clear as water and as smooth as oil,
And no jot knowing of what Maisie knew!
Flushed with the sunset air of roseate Rye
You stand, marmoreal darling of the Few,
Lord of the troubled speech and single Eye.

§ 20

In his own copy of
Caricatures of Twenty-Five Gentlemen

Some dead, some living unremember'd—all
Ruthlessly changed by busybody Time!

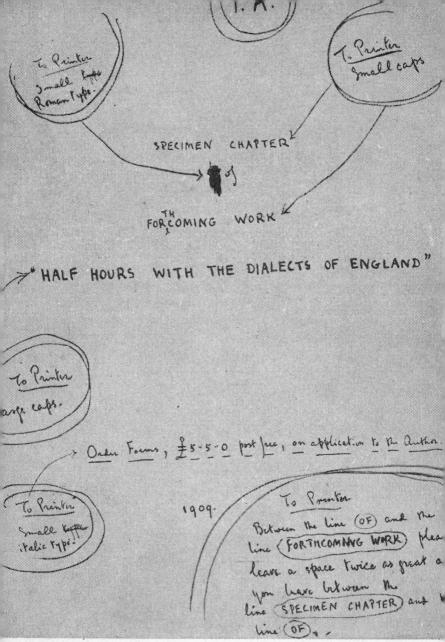

T. A.

To Printer
small ~~type~~
Roman Type.

T. Printer
small caps

SPECIMEN CHAPTER

of

TH
FOR^COMING WORK

"HALF HOURS WITH THE DIALECTS OF ENGLAND"

To Printer
~~l~~arge caps.

Order Forms, £5·5·0 post free, on application to the Author.

1909.

To Printer
small ~~type~~
italic Type.

To Printer
Between the line (OF) and the
line (FORTHCOMING WORK) plea[se]
leave a space twice as great a[s]
you leave between the
line (SPECIMEN CHAPTER) and [the]
line (OF).

The manner in which M. B., an author, dealt with his printer was not sacrosanct to Max, a parodist. Second sheet of the ms. bears the autograph legend *Of this Prospectus 35 copies have been printed (5 of which are for the United States of America). This is No.* , with instruction that it be printed on the title page verso. Reproduced by courtesy of the Harvard College Library.

§ 21. Max's title page and instructions for his 'Specimen Chapter of Forthcoming Work *Half Hours with the Dialects of England*' are reproduced in the plate opposite: here follows the text.

RYE, SUSSEX

Persons passing up the steep and cobbled alley that leads from the main street of this town to Mr. Henry James' residence will have noted on one of the front-doors a small oval brass plate, inscribed thus:

Miss Peploe,

Dressmaker.

The following sonnet was written by none other than Miss Peploe, Dressmaker. It is here reprinted, with the author's sanction, from JAËMES: A ZONNET-ZEQUENCE (privately printed by the Rye Dressmakers' Press).

In the first two lines we have a remarkable instance of the pitfalls which local dialects have for the stranger. A stranger in Rye would jump to the conclusion that Miss Peploe was a highly susceptible woman, on whose heart, however, Mr. James had made no impression at all. In point of fact, Miss Peploe, till Mr. James entered Rye, had been notably impervious to the shafts of Cupid. Her soul had been bounded on the East by her needle, on the West by her yard-measure, on the South by her scissors, and on the North by her thimble. To please her customers had been her sole aspiration.

On the very day of Mr. James' entry into Rye, all was changed. It happened that Miss Peploe was at her window at the moment when he, with the local house-agent, passed up the street to inspect the house where he now resides. As we know, he loved it at first sight. Just so did Miss Peploe love *him*. Since then, it must be confessed, she is not the dressmaker she was. The woman in her has emerged, and the poet become vocal; but the *couturière* leaves much to be desired. Dresses are often not delivered within the time specified. Misfits are frequent. Buttons come off. Seams burst. Customers are angry and few.

Let it be said at once that Mr. James himself is wholly innocent of this sad state of things. It is not, perhaps, likely that a man so observant as he has failed to remark the face of Miss Peploe flying to the window whenever he fares up or down the street. But never has he paused to make sign of recognition. Nor has Miss Peploe, as yet, had the courage or immodesty to tell her secret to him. The sonnet-sequence which she has composed during the past few years, and of which the sonnet here reproduced is the hundred and fifty-third, has never, though addressed to him, been thrust under his eye. It has but been printed privately for circulation among her friends, 'of whom, alas,' as she remarked to the present Editor, ' 'ee do be not för bein' one.' Her book has enjoyed, among the simple townsfolk, a not inconsiderable success. Artless it may be, but it strikes with no uncertain touch the chord of humanity, and has already inspired many other pens, notably that of Peter Jackson, the elderly fisherman whose fine poem about

'The town of Rye, the town of Rye,
Where burning Peploe loves and sings'

will surely have its place in all anthologies of non-dialectic verse. The Editor regrets that Mr. Jackson's classical method excludes him from the 'Half Hours.' In offering to the public the following sample of Miss Peploe's racier Muse, he hopes of it, apart from its importance to the purpose of his book, that it may chance to meet the eye of Mr. James, and so, perhaps, pave the way to Miss Peploe's future happiness.

Jaëmes ! Thou dost be för bein' egregious
To never discommode the heärt o' me
Since thou dost be för 'avin' zitted zee.
Thine eyes do be för bein' glorious,
And thy lips röse-leaves, zürely, which to buss
The whöle broäd world would I för givin' be.
But first o' all, yare, let by Pärson we
Do be för bein' binded, sansy fuss.
I shall do be för gaddin' höme-along
If thou dost be för bein' damsel-coy
O' me. As thou dost be för bein' ztrong,
Do be för bein' merciful. Ahoy !
Wings o' the Dove ! No dove do be för bein'
Möre dove than me when I do thee be zeein'.

LINE 1. *Thou dost be för bein'*: i.e. 'You are.' Throughout history, the inhabitants of Sussex have been noted for their disinclination to commit themselves irrevocably to any one line of policy or school of thought; and this trait in them is well illustrated by their speech. A Sussex man, meeting a friend, does not say, 'How are you ?' and receive the answer 'Very well, thank you.' He says 'Lad, 'ow dost thou be för bein' ?' and the usual answer is, 'I do be för bein' well eno', lad, I do be för thankin' thee.' To the waste of time involved in such modes of speech has been ascribed by many historians the gradual loss of Rye's pre-eminence as a sea-port. (See also the present Editor's pamphlet 'Why Is Brighton No Longer Fashionable ?')

Egregious, a corruption of the Latin *egregius*. The Rye dialect contains many such relics of the old Roman occupation of the city. (cf. *discommode*, line 2.)

LINE 2. *To never discommode.*

What lout soever
In foul Sussex lives
Dares to dissever
His infinitives.
Sing bol-de-rol bol-de-rol lol
Bol-de-rol lol-de-rol lee.

Hampshire Drinking Song.

It is typical of the cautious nature and guarded utterance of the Sussex peasant that he never says he likes a thing. He will but confess that it does not discommode him. 'Polly Zmith do be för bein' egregious to not discommode my heärt' is, from his lips, an outburst of the fieriest lyric passion. It is rarely that a Sussex woman can bring herself to speak in similar terms of a male. Used by almost any other woman than Miss Peploe, such language would be adjudged shameless, in Rye.

LINE 3. *Zitted*, past participle of the verb to zit='to sit,' to reside. *Zee* = here. A corruption of the French word *çi*. One of the numerous Gallicisms which crept into the dialect when Rye was the bright medium for the bulk of England's commerce with France.

LINE 5. *Buss* = kiss. Probably an abbreviation of the Latin word *omnibus*. (See note on *egregious*, line 1.)

LINE 6. Note here the rash hyperbole, so foreign to the Sussex nature. Miss Peploe is not, and never has been, a land-owner. All she could 'för givin' be' is the plant and good-will of her exiguous business. The vastness of her offer is the measure of her infatuation.

LINE 7. *Yare*. A nautical interjection, invented by Shakespeare to give a fillip to Act I, Scene I, of 'The Tempest.' In common use among the inhabitants of Rye. (See note on line 13.)

LINE 8. *Sansy* = without. A corruption of the French word *sans*. (See note on *zee*, line 3.)
Note the subtlety of Miss Peploe's concession to literary agoraphobia.

LINES 9-10. Tourists have taken the threat contained in these two lines as evidence that Miss Peploe and Mr. James had somewhere met and parleyed. Truly 'a little knowledge is a dangerous thing.' In Rye to 'be för gaddin' höme-along' signifies merely to pass away, to go to one's last rest, to die, to be gathered to one's fathers.

LINES 11-12. cf. the hortation so common among Londoners 'As you are strong, be merciful.'

LINE 13. *Wings o' the Dove!* An expletive much favoured by the fishermen of Rye since Mr. James made his home in their midst.

LINES 13-14. Note the Shakespearean dissyllabic rhyme, and the very Shakespearean style and sentiment throughout the couplet. On the strength of these peculiarities, and the difficulty of accounting for them except on the hypothesis that Shakespeare had come to Rye and founded there a tradition of Shakespearean sonneteering, it has been argued by certain local commentators that in Rye, and nowhere else, must have been spent those three years in the poet's life of which there is no apparent record. The present Editor leaves it to wiser heads than his to determine whether or not these commentators do be for being on the right track. He does, however, enter an emphatic *caveat* against the corollary theory that 'Mr. W. H.' was none other than the town of Rye. It would be absurd to call Rye 'Mr. W. H.'

§ 22. Another product of Max's game, this is a sonnet written in 1909 to celebrate the aftermath of M. Louis Blériot's successful airplane flight across the Channel—and evincing a talent that caused certain lines to be excised long before the verses first saw print in 1943.

Lines to be Hung in a Hotel Bedroom at Charing Cross

Remembered Cupid taught dull Man to soar:
I do not wish to but I *must* say more:
Behold the bed on which the Blériots . . .

. . . .

Union of adamant with adipose,
Accentuated by a lack of cloes.
 (The cloes, neglected, lay upon the floor
And passed into the keeping of George Moore.)
So love two earwigs in some battered rose

. . . .

While Emily, sweet creature, gently smiled.
The disproportionate result—one child.

§ 23

Invocation to Luther

Luther ! Thou should'st be with us at this hour;
Thy brawny arms are needed lest we fall
Under the awful and insidious thrall
Of Rome. O come and save us as we cower.
For Lo ! the Pope, like some great poisonous flower
Wafts a base Roman fever over all
And stifles us with what he's pleased to call
His temporal and spiritual power.
The Duke of Norfolk grins in Arundel;
The Marquis d'Hartepoint, like a Brontë witch,
Shrieks through thick clouds of incense fresh from Hell
Strange Latin Psalms and incantations weird.
Come, step down, Luther, from your whitewashed niche
And let the earth be cleaned, the air be cleared.

Rapallo

1910-1915

§ 24

In Max's top hat

Once I used to perch on Max Beerbohm's pate,
But now he's become Italianate;
So here in contempt and disregard
I moulder for ever at Appletree Yard.

§ 25

In a letter to Edmund Gosse

I do love to watch Lady Speyer
Mount higher and higher and higher,
    Altho' I am fond
    Of poor Lady Mond—
And also of poor Lady Meyer.

§ 26

The Characters of Shakespeare

Charles Lamb and Samuel Taylor C.,
Schlegel and Dowden and Sidney Lee—
They one and all of them seem to me
    To take too hard
    The work of the Bard.
Simpler modes appeal to me.
Return we to simpler modes.—M. B.

There once was a king named Macbeth;
A better king never drew breath;
 The faults of his life
 Were all due to his wife,
The notorious *Lady* Macbeth.

No doubt you have heard of Othello—
An African sort of a fellow.
 When they said 'You are black!'
 He cried 'Take it back!
I am only an exquisite yellow.'

I cannot help feeling that Lear
At the end of his splendid career,
 When he strolled in the teeth
 Of that storm on that heath,
Was—well, just a little bit 'queer.'

Hamlet, I'm sorry to find,
Was unable to make up his mind;
 He shillied, he shallied,
 He dillied, he dallied—
In fact, he was over-refined.

Then Cymbeline. How about Cymbeline?
You could hold in a cup—in a thimble, e'en—
 All that is not
 Sheer downright *rot*
In Shakespeare's presentment of Cymbeline.

The doings of Coriolanus
Shall not for one moment detain us.
 It's clear that we can't
 And we won't and we shan't
Be bothered with Coriolanus.

Hats off, however, to Romeo—
One o' the Montagues, don't-you-know;
     And we mustn't forget
     That dear little pet
     Of the Capulet set,
          Juliet,
Who asked him *why* he was Romeo.

The other Shakespearean characters
Are deadly damned dullards and dodderers.
     I would warn you to shun
     Every one
Of the other Shakespearean characters.

These simpler modes appeal to me,
Though very repellent to E. G. C.,
My dear old neighbour and friend.—M. B.

§ 27. This fragment, and that in 28, are the only reproduced works from the vast multilingual output of the Duke of Dorset. Here, spurred by Zuleika Dobson's heartlessness, he inveighs against Woman as a warning to his heir—

Epistle by the Duke to his heir presumptive

Vae tibi, vae misero, nisi circumspexeris artes
Femineas, nam nulla salus quin femina possit
Tradere, nulla fides quin——

§ 28. So great was the Duke's sense of *noblesse oblige* that he took time from envisioning his suicide—and substituted the English equivalent for the Greek he preferred—to pen a testimonial to his landlady's cooking and lodging—

To an Undergraduate Needing Rooms in Oxford

(A Sonnet in Oxfordshire Dialect)

Zeek w'ere thee will in t'Univürsity,
Lad, thee'll not vind nör bread nör bed that matches
Them as thee'll vind, roight züre, at Mrs. Batch's . . .

§ 29

After Hilaire Belloc

One Christmas Night in Pontgibaud
    (Pom-pom, rub-a-dub-dub)
A man with a drum went to and fro
    (Two merry eyes, two cheeks chub)
Nor not a citril within, without,
But heard the racket and heard the rout
And marvelled what it was all about
    (And who shall shrive Beelzebub?)

He whacked so hard the drum was split
    (Pom-pom, rub-a-dub-dum)
Out lept Saint Gabriel from it
    (Præclarissimus Omnium)

Who spread his wings and up he went
Nor ever paused in his ascent
Till he had reached the firmament
    (*Benedicamus Dominum*).

§ 30

Again—after Hilaire Belloc

At dawn to-morrow
    On Storrington Barrow
I'll beg or borrow
    A bow and arrow
And shoot sleek sorrow
    Through the marrow.
The floods are out and the ford is narrow,
The stars hang dead and my limbs are lead,
    But ale is gold
    And there's good foot-hold
On the Cuckfield side of Storrington Barrow.

§ 31

A Sequelula to *The Dynasts*[1]

The Void is disclosed. Our own Solar System is visible, distant by
some two million miles.

Enter the Ancient Spirit and Chorus of the Years, the Spirit and
Chorus of the Pities, the Spirit Ironic, the Spirit Sinister,
Rumours, Spirit-Messengers, and the Recording Angel.

SPIRIT OF THE PITIES

Yonder, that swarm of things insectual
Wheeling Nowhither in Particular—
What is it?

SPIRIT OF THE YEARS

That? Oh that is merely one
Of those innumerous congeries
Of parasites by which, since time began,
Space has been interfested.

SPIRIT SINISTER

What a pity
We have no means of stamping out these pests!

SPIRIT IRONIC

Nay, but I like to watch them buzzing round,
Poor little trumpery ephaeonals!

---

1. This has been composed from a scenario thrust on me by some one
else. My philosophy of life saves me from sense of responsibility for any
of my writings; but I venture to hold myself specially irresponsible for
this one.—Th*m*s H*rdy.

CHORUS OF THE PITIES

(aerial music)

Yes, yes!
What matter a few more or less?
   Here and Nowhere plus
   Whence and Why makes Thus.
   Let these things be.
There's room in the world for them and us.
   Nothing is,

Out in the vast immensities
   Where these things flit,
   Irrequisite
   In a minor key
To the tune of the sempiternal It.

SPIRIT IRONIC

The curious thing about them is that some
Have lesser parasites adherent to them—
Bipedular and quadrupedular
Infinitesimals. On close survey
You see these movesome. Do you not recall,
We once went in a party and beheld
All manner of absurd things happening
On one of those same—planets, don't you call them?

SPIRIT OF THE YEARS

(screwing up his eyes at the Solar System)

One of that very swarm it was, if I mistake not.
It had a parasite that called itself
Napoléon. And lately, I believe,
Another parasite has had the impudence
To publish an elaborate account
Of our (for so we deemed it) private visit.

SPIRIT SINISTER

His name?

RECORDING ANGEL

One moment.

(Turns over leaves)

Hardy, Mr. Thomas,
Novelist. Author of 'The Woodlanders,'
'Far from the Madding Crowd,' 'The Trumpet Major,'
'Tess of the D'Urbervilles,' etcetera,
Etcetera. In 1895
'Jude the Obscure' was published, and a few
Hasty reviewers, having to supply
A column for the day of publication,
Filled out their space by saying that there were
Several passages that might have been
Omitted with advantage. Mr. Hardy
Saw that if that was so, well then, of course,
Obviously the only thing to do
Was to write no more novels, and forthwith
Applied himself to drama and to Us.

SPIRIT IRONIC

Let us hear what he said about Us.

THE OTHER SPIRITS

Let's.

RECORDING ANGEL

(raising receiver of aerial telephone)

3 oh 4 double oh 5, Space. . . . Hulloa.
Is that the Superstellar Library?

I'm the Recording Angel. Kindly send me
By Spirit-Messenger a copy of
'The Dynasts' by T. Hardy. Thank you.

A pause. Enter Spirit-Messenger, with copy of 'The Dynasts.'

Thanks.

Exit Spirit-Messenger. The Recording Angel reads 'The Dynasts'
aloud.

Just as the reading draws to a close, enter the Spirit of Mr. Clement
Shorter and Chorus of Subtershorters. They are visible as small
grey transparencies swiftly interpenetrating the brains of the
spatial Spirits.

SPIRIT OF THE PITIES

It is a book which, once you take it up,
You cannot readily lay down.

SPIRIT SINISTER
There is
Not a dull page in it.

SPIRIT OF THE YEARS
A bold conception
Outcarried with that artistry for which
The author's name is guarantee. We have
No hesitation in commending to our readers
A volume which—

The Spirit of Mr. Clement Shorter and Chorus of Subtershorters are
detected and expelled.

—we hasten to denounce
As giving an entirely false account
Of our impressions.

SPIRIT IRONIC

Hear, *hear!*

SPIRIT SINISTER

Hear, *hear!*

SPIRIT OF THE PITIES

Hear!

SPIRIT OF THE YEARS

Intensive vision has this Mr. Hardy,
With a dark skill in weaving word-patterns
Of subtle ideographies that mark him
A man of genius. So am not I,
But a plain Spirit, simple and forthright,
With no damned philosophical fal-lals
About me. When I visited that planet
And watched the animalcula thereon,
I never said they were 'automata'
And 'jackaclocks,' nor dared describe their deeds
As 'Life's Impulsion by Incognizance.'
It may be that those mites have no free will,
But how should I know? Nay, how Mr. Hardy?
We cannot glimpse the origin of things,
Cannot conceive a Causeless Cause, albeit
Such a Cause must have been, and must be greater
Than we whose little wits cannot conceive it.
'Incognizance'! Why deem incognizant
An infinitely higher than ourselves?
How dare define its way with us? How know
Whether it leaves us free or holds us bond?

SPIRIT OF THE PITIES

Allow me to associate myself
With every word that's fallen from your lips.
The author of 'The Dynasts' has indeed
Misused his undeniably great gifts
In striving to belittle things that are
Little enough already. I don't say
That the phrenetical behaviour
Of those aforesaid animalcula
Did, while we watched them, seem to indicate
Possession of free-will. But, bear in mind,
We saw them in peculiar circumstances—
At war, blinded with blood and lust and fear.
Is it not likely that at other times
They are quite decent midgets, capable
Of thinking for themselves, and also acting
Discreetly on their own initiative,
Not drilled and herded, yet gregarious—
A wise yet frolicsome community?

SPIRIT IRONIC

What are these 'other times' though? I had thought
Those midgets whiled away the vacuous hours
After one war in training for the next.
And let me add that my contempt for them
Is not done justice to by Mr. Hardy.

SPIRIT SINISTER

Nor mine. And I have reason to believe
Those midgets shone above their average
When we inspected them.

A RUMOUR
(tactfully intervening)

> *Yet have I heard*
(Though not on very good authority)
That once a year they hold a festival
And thereat all with one accord unite
In brotherly affection and good will.

SPIRIT OF THE YEARS
(to Recording Angel)

Can you authenticate this Rumour?

RECORDING ANGEL

Such festival they have, and call it 'Christmas.'

SPIRIT OF THE PITIES

Then let us go and reconsider them
Next 'Christmas.'

SPIRIT OF THE YEARS
(to Recording Angel)

> *When is that?*

RECORDING ANGEL
(consults terrene calendar)

> *This day three weeks.*

SPIRIT OF THE YEARS

On that day we will re-traject ourselves.
Meanwhile, 'twere well we should be posted up
In details of this feast.

SPIRIT OF THE PITIES
(to Recording Angel)

Aye, tell us more.

RECORDING ANGEL

I fancy you could best find what you need
In the Complete Works of the late Charles Dickens.
I have them here.

SPIRIT OF THE YEARS

Read them aloud to us.

The Recording Angel reads aloud the Complete Works of Charles
Dickens.

RECORDING ANGEL
(closing 'Edwin Drood')

'Tis Christmas Morning.

SPIRIT OF THE YEARS

Then must we away.

SEMICHORUS I. OF YEARS
(aerial music)

'Tis time we press on to revisit
That dear little planet,
To-day of all days to be seen at
Its brightest and best.

Now holly and mistletoe girdle
Its halls and its homesteads,
And every biped is beaming
With peace and good will.

SEMICHORUS II.

With good will and why not with free will?
If clearly the former

May nest in those bosoms, then why not
*   The latter as well?*

Let's lay down no laws to trip up on,
*   Our way is in darkness,*
And not but by groping unhampered
*   We win to the light.*

The Spirit and Chorus of the Years traject themselves, closely followed by the Spirit and Chorus of the Pities, the Spirits and Choruses Sinister and Ironic, Rumours, Spirit-Messengers, and the Recording Angel.

There is the sound of a rushing wind. The Solar System is seen for a few instants growing larger and larger—a whorl of dark, vastening orbs careering round the sun. All but one of these is lost to sight. The convex seas and continents of our planet spring into prominence.

The Spirit of Mr. Hardy is visible as a grey transparency swiftly interpenetrating the brain of the Spirit of the Years, and urging him in a particular direction, to a particular point.

The Aerial Visitants now hover in mid-air on the outskirts of Casterbridge, Wessex, immediately above the County Gaol.

SPIRIT OF THE YEARS

First let us watch the revelries within
This well-kept castle whose great walls connote
A home of the pre-eminently blest.

The roof of the gaol becomes transparent, and the whole interior is revealed, like that of a beehive under glass.

Warders are marching mechanically round the corridors of white stone, unlocking and clanging open the iron doors of the cells. Out from every door steps a convict, who stands at attention, his face to the wall.

At a word of command the convicts fall into gangs of twelve, and
 march down the stone stairs, out into the yard, where they line
 up against the walls.

Another word of command, and they file mechanically, but not more
 mechanically than their warders, into the Chapel.

SPIRIT OF THE PITIES

Enough!

SPIRITS SINISTER AND IRONIC
'Tis more than even we can bear.

SPIRIT OF THE PITIES

Would we had never come!

SPIRIT OF THE YEARS
Brother, 'tis well

To have faced a truth however hideous,
However humbling. Gladly I discipline
My pride by taking back those pettish doubts
Cast on the soundness of the central thought
In Mr. Hardy's drama. He was right.
Automata these animalcula
Are—puppets, pitiable jackaclocks.
Be 't as it may elsewhere, upon this planet
There's no free will, only obedience
To some blind, deaf, unthinking despotry
That justifies the horridest pessimism.
Frankly acknowledging all this, I beat
A quick but not disorderly retreat.

He re-trajects himself into Space, followed closely by his Chorus, and
 by the Spirit and Chorus of the Pities, the Spirits Sinister and
 Ironic with their Choruses, Rumours, Spirit-Messengers, and the
 Recording Angel.

§ 32

Ballade of an Illustrious Freshman

The University of Oxford hails
    In awe not quite this side idolatry
His Royal Highness, Edward, Prince of Wales
    (With whom is Mr. Hansell). *'Pueri*
    Senesque plaudunt,' and in ecstasy
The President of Magdalen's eye dilates
    At sight of him who shall henceforth supply
A model to all undergraduates.

In every duty that his lot entails
    He had been coached with assiduity.
A sea-dog once, on land he never fails
    To exercise that midship modesty
    Which is what always and especially
The unsleeping Mr. Hansell cultivates
    To make this lad's impeccability
A model to all undergraduates.

Yet cars shall skid, and trams go off their rails,
    And horses curvet, as he treads the High,
And Proctors fawn, and Bull-Dogs wag their tails,
    And oh good heavens ! the anxiety
    When Mr. Hansell, very gingerly
Begins to pick for him his intimates,
    Each one of whom shall be vicariously
A model to all undergraduates.

ENVOI

Prince ! (Mr. Hansell, stand aside, please.) Try
To do just as your winged young soul dictates,
And (Silence ! Mr. Hansell) be thereby
A model to all undergraduates.

§ 33

Elegy on Any Lady
by
George Moore

That she adored me as the most
    Adorable of males
I think I may securely boast.
    Dead women tell no tales.

§ 34. This is the *œuvre* said to have delayed Max's knighthood for twenty years:

Ballade Tragique à Double Refrain

SCENE: A Room in Windsor Castle   TIME: The Present

Enter a Lady-in-Waiting and a Lord-in-Waiting

SHE: Slow pass the hours—ah, passing slow !
    My doom is worse than anything
Conceived by Edgar Allan Poe:
    The Queen is duller than the King.

HE: Lady, your mind is wandering;
You babble what you do not mean.
    Remember, to your heartening,
The King is duller than the Queen.

SHE: No, most emphatically No !
    To one firm-rooted fact I cling
In my now chronic vertigo:
    The Queen is duller than the King.

HE: Lady, you lie. Last evening
I found him with a Rural Dean,
    Talking of district-visiting . . .
The King is duller than the Queen.

SHE: At any rate he doesn't sew !
    You don't see *him* embellishing
Yard after yard of calico . . .
    The Queen is duller than the King.
    Oh to have been an underling
To (say) the Empress Josephine !

HE: Enough of your self-pitying!
              The King is duller than the Queen.

SHE *(firmly)*: The Queen is duller than the King.

HE: Death then for you shall have no sting.

              [*Stabs her and, as she falls dead, produces phial
              from breast-pocket of coat.*]

              Nevertheless, sweet friend Strychnine,
                  [*Drinks.*]

              The King—is—duller than——the Queen.

              [*Dies in terrible agony.*]

§ 35. Could Enoch Soames have owed more than he acknowledged to
the young French—and English—décadents? From *Fungoids*, his second
volume:

To a Young Woman

Thou art, who hast not been!
    Pale tunes irresolute
    And traceries of old sounds
    Blown from a rotted flute
Mingle with noise of cymbals rouged with rust,
Nor not strange forms and epicene
    Lie bleeding in the dust,
        Being wounded with wounds.

        For this it is
    That in thy counterpart
        Of age-long mockeries
Thou hast not been nor art!

§ 36. Enoch Soames, the Catholic Diabolist, in rollicking change-of-pace; also from *Fungoids*.

Nocturne

Round and round the shutter'd Square
I stroll'd with the Devil's arm in mine.
No sound but the scrape of his hoofs was there
And the ring of his laughter and mine.
  We had drunk black wine.

I scream'd, 'I will race you, Master!'
'What matter,' he shriek'd, 'to-night
Which of us runs the faster?
There is nothing to fear to-night
  In the foul moon's light!'

Then I look'd him in the eyes,
And I laugh'd full shrill at the lie he told
And the gnawing fear he would fain disguise.
It was true, what I'd time and again been told:
  He was old—old.

§ 37

Drinking Song

In days of yore the Drama throve
    Within our storm-bound coasts,
The Independent Theatre gave
    Performances of 'Ghosts.'
Death and disease, disaster
    And downfall were our joy,
The fun flew fast and faster
While Ibsen was our Master
    And Grein was a bright Dutch boy, my boys,
    And Grein was a bright Dutch boy.

Then, oh, just wasn't Sudermann
    A name to conjure with?
Echegaray to us was kin,
    And Björnson Björnson kith.
We said aloud, 'The Stage is
    The thing that shall employ
The faculties of Sages
And Heirs of *all* the Ages,'
    When Grein was a bright Dutch boy, my boys,
    When Grein was a bright Dutch boy.

The Future of the Drama
    Was our theme day in, day out,
Pinero was most sanguine,
    Henry Arthur had no doubt.
'On, on!' cried William Archer,
    And no man was less coy

Than Shaw, that spring-heel'd marcher
In *any* new deparcher,
>   When Grein was a bright Dutch boy, my boys,
>   When Grein was a bright Dutch boy.

The Movies moved not yet, my boys,
>   Revues were not in view,
The present state of things was not
>   Foreseen by me and you.
We sailed o'er seas uncharted
>   Of youth and faith and joy.
None cried 'Are we downhearted ?'
In those dear days departed
>   When Grein was a bright Dutch boy, my boys,
>   When Grein was a bright Dutch boy.

§ 38

A Ballade of Judges

A student of sociology
    (Using that word in its finer sense),
Bien vu by the governing classes, I
    Have met most persons of Consequence
Round one and another mahogany:
Bishops, Diplomats, Literary
    Gents, Proconsuls——in fine
The pick of the whole community . . .
    But where do the *Judges* dine?

I cannot accept the theory
    That they simply abstain from sustinence.
In every Court diurnally
    At one of the clock My Lord goes hence
Through dim green curtains to privacy
For a full half-hour. Which things imply
    That a chop and a glass of wine
Are used to stoke his mentality.
    But where do the Judges *dine?*

Are they never asked out? Or are they shy?
    We know their daily magnificence
Of ermined and horse-haired panoply
    Flaunted regardless of all expense.
Why don't we know their shirt-fronts? Why

Even in old sad Bloomsbury
    Do they never toe the line ?
They must dine somewhere, obviously;
    But *where* do the Judges dine ?

ENVOI

Stars ! in the matter of whither and whence
You are wheeling I ask no sign;
I never commit an impertinence;
But—*Where do the Judges dine ?*

§ 39

In a copy of More's

(or Shaw's or Wells's or Plato's or anybody's)

Utopia

So this is Utopia, is it ? Well
I beg your pardon, I thought it was Hell.

§ 40

Mr. John Masefield

A swear-word in a rustic slum
A simple swear-word is to some,
    To Masefield something more.

§ 41

A Ballade of My Betters

Gold, being golden, jars on zinc,
    And crystal scratches common clay.
I, who am ordinary, shrink
    From men whose footsteps never stray
    And heavenward brook no delay.
By any such an one I'm riled
    And with an ill-bred sneer I say,
'You must have been an awful child.'

There's no expenditure of ink
    By which my stylo could convey
How great a Moral Force I think
    Campbell (the Reverend R. J.).
    Yet when he flashes forth his ray
Of New Theology (so styled)
    I murmur, 'Be that as it may,
You must have been an awful child.'

There's something wrong with me, I think.
    As often as Sir Edward Grey,
With Europe trembling on the brink
    Of Armageddon, says his say
    In his cold, strong, sweet, wise, right way,
I have an impulse strange and wild
    To shout 'You dear old popinjay
You must have been an awful child.'

ENVOI

Milton, my help, my prop, my stay,
My well of English undefiled,
It struck me suddenly today
You must have been *an awful* child.

· 55 ·

§ 42

On the Uniform Edition of the works of George Meredith

'Here lie the bones of Richard Feverel.'
'Have you any other editions?' 'Several.'
'Then I'd rather have one of *them*, please. I've
A sort of a feeling for Richard alive.'

§ 43

On the Uniform Edition of the works of Henry James

Here fair young Daisy Miller lies.
O, Speculator, pass not by!
What though her spirit will not rise?
Her tomb's price will, quite possibly.

§ 44

On the Uniform Edition of the works of R. L. Stevenson

'*Ci-gît*——who? You'll never guess!'
'Gibbon perhaps?' 'No; R. L. S.'
'He?——that blithe adventurer? He?
Well, poor fellow, R. I. P.'

§ 45

A Ballade *ad hoc*

You can always find plenty of things to do.
    But—things worth doing? Seldom one,
And still more seldom so many as two.
    Writing Ballades is rather fun,
    Villanelles do harm to none,
And Triolets never have led to crime
    Or made 'men's children curse the sun'—
But what an appalling waste of time!

Despite the agony I go through
    In getting a metre to trip and run
By the aid of an ear not over-true,
    Writing Ballades is rather fun;
    And this time, surely, with bun, gun, spun,
    And won—to say nothing of dun and ton—
    And even ruling out Eckermann—
I've hit on an easy central rhyme;
    And I mean to hang on till my course is run.
But *what* an appalling waste of time!

There were good songs written by Brian Boru,
    And I seem to remember a Portuguese Nun
Who wrote Robert Browning a sonnet or two.
    Writing Ballades is rather fun
    If you drag in anything under the sun

And care not a fig if it all——Well, I'm
    Blowed if my job isn't nearly done,
But what an *appalling* waste of time !

ENVOI

'Tention, Prince ! The envoi's begun.
Writing Ballades is rather fun.
And always receiving 'em must be prime—
But *what* an *appalling* waste of time !

§ 46

To W. S.——1914

Walter, how skill'd a conjurer Time is !
In my green boyhood I regarded you
As old, quite old. Your talk was my dear clue
To far-off faint romantic mysteries—
Frank Miles's ladies, Whistler's Symphonies,
Justin's ambitions, Irving's 'Much Ado,'
And all that Leybourne's lungs sent throbbing through
The Hoxton Palace of Varieties.
Now that I'm old and grey (though still quite clever)
You're an authentic juvenile, and few things
Warm my heart more than to perceive you ever
Nailing your flag to some unseason'd mast—
A doer of the newest of the new things,
And deem'd unruly by the boys of 'Blast.'

Far Oakridge

1915-1919

§ 47. The Beerbohms took a cottage on the Rothensteins' farm at Far Oakridge during World War I, and there Max celebrated a lively member of his friends' ménage.

Brave Rover

Rover killed the goat,
He bit him through the throat,
And when it all was over
The goat's ghost haunted Rover.

And yet (the plot here thickens)
Rover killed the chickens.
They thought he was a fox—
And then he killed the cocks.

And now events moved faster:
Rover killed his master,
And then he took the life
Of his late master's wife.

And we must not forget he
Killed Rachel and killed Bettie,
Then Billie and then John.
How dogs do carry on!

To Bradford he repaired.
His great white teeth he bared
And then, with awful snarls,
Polished off Uncle Charles.

Albert in London trembled—
An aspen he resembled—
His life he held not cheap
And wept. (I heard him weep.)

Brave Rover heard him too.
He knew full well who's who,
And entered with a grin
The Fields of Lincoln's Inn.

The Elysian Fields begin
Near those of Lincoln's Inn.
'Tis there that Albert's gone.
How dogs do carry on !

§ 48

Thomas Hardy and A. E. Housman

How compare either of this grim twain ?
    Each has an equal knack,
Hardy prefers the pill that's blue,
    Housman the draught that's black.

§ 49. With William Rothenstein as a partner, the sonnet game reached
peak production: this and the series of five selections following were
composed from 1915 until the War's end. Lines 2, 5, 8, 11 and 14
are Max's.

To Rabindranath Tagore

Tagore, the nature once so clean we knew
Before you sailed from India's coral strand
That nature once we thought to understand
Is now become a thing for fashion's view,
Equivocal in form, subfusc in hue,
Obnoxious to the scent, a thing to brand.
What might it yet have been had not this land
Unfortunately made a pet of you?
Now turn a turbid ear to what I fain
Would tell you while there is yet time and hope.
Could'st thou but be a bright black boy again
Along the Ganges ghats where many a corpse
Would caution thee and tell thee to use soap
As do the Orpens (sometimes called the Orps).

§ 50. The even-numbered lines are by Max, the odd-numbered ones by William Rothenstein.

Iles Farm, Far Oakridge

Beerbohm, thine eye is flecked with Saturn's rays,
But Hermes' brow is not so fair as thine
When the whole firmament doth seem to blaze
Like Zeppelins o'er Newcastle-on-Tyne.
Go cleanse thine eye that it may look once more
Upon that City of the Violet Crown
Far Oakridge called; but now a-troubled sore
By autumn's slow demise in red and brown.
Take up thy pen. Now smite with coward blow
The base usurper of that farm which Iles
Built with his own strong hands, now fall'n so low.
Pursue him ruthlessly o'er fields and stiles
With lying wads and meretricious stroke
And rid the district of his loathsome yoke.

§ 51.   Odd lines are Max's, even lines are Rothenstein's.

To the Rev. Percy Dearmer

Dearmer ! Your beard would be a royal blue
Were you to turn your face towards Krishna's land
(Commonly known as 'India's Coral Strand')
To gild it with thy missionary glue.
Methinks the P. and O. boat's very screw
Doth make more lily still thy lily hand
And thy bland voice more clerically bland
Since thou wast joined again in wedlock true.
Thou art the poison Krishna drained for us,
Thou art the shame he lifted from our brows.
And shalt thou yet, foul spawn of Erebus,
Defile the land made sacred by Tagore ?
That black man's harem does not need *thy* spouse.
Hide thy black face, and her white face the more.

§ 52. The blithe cross-purposes of the odd lines would indicate, almost without the verification from handwriting, Max's authorship; even lines are Rothenstein's.

Frau Krupp's 'little dears'

Once, standing on a peak in Darien,
I watched the bombs falling like morning dew
Freshly, alike on Gentile and on Jew
Scatt'ring alike the wary and unwary one—
All of the Terrys, not excepting Marion—
And thought, how wrong the act, how right the view,
And aptly quoted Horace's 'Eheu.'
Alas, I cried, O period Arthurian
Which Tennyson hath made for ever smug,
How poor a thing Excalibur appears,
And Lancelot himself a kind of slug,
Beside these marvels of our happier days.
These bolts, which Frau Krupp calls her little dears,
Tear from the brow of Homer all his bays.

§ 53. Even lines by Max, odd ones by Rothenstein.

Eli the Thatcher

O thou whose name shatters the universe,
Eli, old thatcher who in long-gone days
Thatched other heads than mine, whose puny verse
Totters along like an old man in stays.
What stories of these hills hast thou to tell!
Stories of sheep that turned their fangs on men,
Of rabbits that could cast their awful spell
Even on poachers and two-headed calves!
Tell us some story now, to rouse our blood,
Of that old Squire whose son you cut in halves,
Of ladies roasted, babies cooked in mud—
Come, greybeard, rouse yourself, and let none say
You have forgot to tread the ancient way.

§ 54. A third hand played the sonnet game here, but Max's lines are 3, 6, 9 and 12.

To Max

on his taking his only walk at Oakridge

O Max when stepping forth into the close
You met brave Rover coming from his walk
Across the prostrate corpse of Miss Kate Rorke
Prinked out in Rosalind's once spotless hose;
And Rover deigning not to soil his toes
On what he fancied was old cold roast pork
Invited you to bark, but not to talk.
She bounded up and hit him on the nose.
I, who am privy to her hideous past,
O Max, what could I whisper in thine ear!
I will not tell you of that hideous last
Attempt of hers to blackmail our dear King
Turning his life into a thing of fear.
For Max indeed has walking lost its sting.

§ 55

On the origin of the name *Cirencester*

In Early Anglo-Saxon days
A beauteous damsel lived near here.
She was, in Pre-Chaucerian phrase,
'A verrie parfitt gentil deare.'

Ah, had he but been living then,
She'd have been sung of by Lord Byron.
Women disparaged her, but men
Adored her. She was called The Siren.

Now, names weren't common in those rough
Archaic days of which I sing.
HE, SHE, and IT were good enough
For almost any one or thing.

The owner of this very farm
Was not called Iles. Addressed as such,
He would have felt profound alarm
And have disliked you very much.

For he himself, his ass, his ox,
His son-in-law and sub-lessee,
His masculine pigs, his rams and cocks,
Were ev'ry one of them called HE.

His wife, you may depend upon 't,
His serving-wench, his daughters three,
Had all been christened at the font
(If any fonts existed) SHE.

Iᴛ was his roof, his bed of straw,
The rain, the snow, the evening star,
Fish, flesh and fowl, beak, tooth and claw—
Iᴛ, you'll agree, went rather far.

Iᴛ (as they called the march of Time)
Produced in men a wish to try
To differentiate—and I'm
Not slow to guess the reason why.

I guess all things were in confusion—
Women and hens, and men and asses,
Reality and gross illusion,
The upper and the lower classes.

Henceforth men called a spade a spade
And called a man a man for a' that,
A wood a wood, a glade a glade,
A warming pan a pan for a' that.

One man was Dick, another Garge,
Etcetera, etcetera,
And social intercourse at large
Grew easier and betterer.

Surnames crept in—Smiths, Joneses, Browns,
And Rothensteins, and—I'll be blowed!—
Even on villages and towns
Distinctive names were now bestowed.

The town in which the Siren dwelt—
I hope you've not forgot the Siren—
Her whose transcendent charms could melt
Like wax the hearts of men of iron—

Well—to resume—the town where she
Hung out in (let us call it) maid-
-en meditation fancy-free,
But sprightlier in her mien than staid—

This town—to re-resume—was still,
In all the maps and things, called IT.
The townsmen met, and cried 'We ill
Deserve this slight. It hurts a bit.

It jars. It irks. It's apt to pall.
It cries to heaven. It seems a pity.
Remember! we are, hang it all,
The citizens of no mean city.'—

(A slight exaggeration p'raps,
But I am not pedantic—
These were not clear cold classic chaps
But lovably romantic.)

The Siren heard the noise without
And leaned forth from her window-frame.
The men received her with a shout
And straightway cried 'By thy dear name

Henceforward let our town be called !—
'Siren'—the very thing—first-rate—
Straightforward without being bald—
Brief and direct, yet delicate.'

No doubt, but ah ! the hasty throng
Reckoned without its womenkind.
The women bade it move along
And gave it bits of their own mind.

Yet, tho' they brush'd the men aside
With heaving breasts and flashing eyes,
You'll find they soon exemplified
The British love of compromise.

I should have told you long ago
The Siren had a sister, Jane—
Nice and well-meaning, don't you know,
But quite unfortunately plain.

It was in her the women saw
The basis for a settlement.
'Gents,' they proclaimed, 'our word is law,
We hereby close this incident.

The Siren's vile renown shall not
Go rolling down the Future's vista.
'Tention ! Eyes front ! We name this spot
Now and for ever SIREN'S SISTER.'

§ 56

Lines on a certain Friend's remarkable Faculty for swift Generalisation

'How do you do ?' Will asked of me.
'Very well, thanks,' said I. Said he,
'Yes, I invariably find
Abundant health in all mankind.'

Next morning, 'How d'you do ?' asked Will.
I said that I was rather ill.
'Alas,' his voice toll'd like a bell,
'Mankind was ever far from well.'

§ 57

Same Cottage—but Another Song, of Another Season

Morning and night I found
White snow upon the ground,
And on the tragic well
Grey ice had cast its spell.
A dearth of wood and coal
Lay heavy on my soul.

My garden was a scene
Of weeds and nettles green,
My window-panes had holes
Through which, all night, lost souls
Peered from the desert road,
And starved cocks faintly crowed.

My path of cinders black
Had an abundant lack
Of visitors, till time
Bade us with boxes climb
The train that hurries on
To old warm Paddington.

§ 58

After W. B. Yeats

From the lone hills where Fergus strays
Down the long vales of Coonahan
Comes a white wind through the unquiet ways,
And a tear shall lead the blind man.

§ 59. Ladbroke Brown's untimely death under the wheels of a motor-omnibus in Piccadilly Circus obliged Max, his literary executor, to provide a scenario for Act V and so enable the masterpiece to be judged as a whole.

SAVONAROLA

A TRAGEDY

by

L. BROWN

ACT I

SCENE: *A Room in the Monastery of San Marco, Florence.*

TIME: 1490, A.D. *A summer morning.*

Enter the SACRISTAN *and a* FRIAR.

SACR.
Savonarola looks more grim to-day
Than ever. Should I speak my mind, I'd say
That he was fashioning some new great scourge
To flay the backs of men.

FRI.
                  'Tis even so.
Brother Filippo saw him stand last night

In solitary vigil till the dawn
Lept o'er the Arno, and his face was such
As men may wear in Purgatory—nay,
E'en in the inmost core of Hell's own fires.

SACR.

I often wonder if some woman's face,
Seen at some rout in his old worldling days,
Haunts him e'en now, e'en here, and urges him
To fierier fury 'gainst the Florentines.

FRI.

Savonarola love-sick ! Ha, ha, ha !
Love-sick ? He, love-sick ? 'Tis a goodly jest !
The *con*firm'd misogyn a ladies' man !
Thou must have eaten of some strange red herb
That takes the reason captive. I will swear
Savonarola never yet hath seen
A woman but he spurn'd her. Hist ! He comes.

  [*Enter* SAVONAROLA, *rapt in thought.*]

Give thee good morrow, Brother.

SACR.

      And therewith
A multitude of morrows equal-good
Till thou, by Heaven's grace, hast wrought the work
Nearest thine heart.

SAV.

    I thank thee, Brother, yet
I thank thee not, for that my thankfulness
(An such there be) gives thanks to Heav'n alone.

FRI. [*To* SACR.]

'Tis a right answer he hath given thee.
Had Sav'narola spoken less than thus,
Methinks me, the less Sav'narola he.
As when the snow lies on yon Apennines,
White as the hem of Mary Mother's robe,
And insusceptible to the sun's rays,
Being harder to the touch than temper'd steel,
E'en so this great gaunt monk white-visagèd
Upstands to Heaven and to Heav'n devotes
The scarpèd thoughts that crown the upper slopes
Of his abrupt and *aus*tere nature.

SACR.

                          Aye.

[*Enter* LUCREZIA BORGIA, ST. FRANCIS OF ASSISI, *and* LEONARDO
DA VINCI. LUC. *is thickly veiled.*]

ST. FRAN.

This is the place.

LUC. [*Pointing at* SAV.]

                    And this the man ! [*Aside.*] And I—
By the hot blood that courses i' my veins
I swear it ineluctably—the woman !

SAV.

Who is this wanton ?

　　[LUC. *throws back her hood, revealing her face.* SAV. *starts
　　back, gazing at her.*]

ST. FRAN.

                    Hush, Sir ! 'Tis my little sister

· 76 ·

The poisoner, right well-belov'd by all
Whom she as yet hath spared. Hither she came
Mounted upon another little sister of mine—
A mare, caparison'd in goodly wise.
She—I refer now to Lucrezia—
Desireth to have word of thee anent
Some matter that befrets her.

SAV. [*To* LUC.]

                Hence ! Begone !
Savonarola will not tempted be
By face of woman e'en tho' 't be, tho' 'tis,
Surpassing fair. All hope abandon therefore.
I charge thee: Vade retro, Satanas !

LEONARDO
Sirrah, thou speakst in haste, as is the way
Of monkish men. The beauty of Lucrezia
Commends, not discommends, her to the eyes
Of keener thinkers than I take thee for.
I am an artist and an engineer,
Giv'n o'er to subtile dreams of what shall be
On this our planet. I foresee a day
When men shall skim the earth i' certain chairs
Not drawn by horses but sped on by oil
Or other matter, and shall thread the sky
Birdlike.

LUC.
      It may be as thou sayest, friend,
Or may be not. [*To* SAV.] As touching this our errand,
I crave of thee, Sir Monk, an audience
Instanter.

FRI.

Lo ! Here Alighieri comes.
I had methought me he was still at Parma.

[*Enter* DANTE.]

ST. FRAN. [*To* DAN.]
How fares my little sister Beatrice ?

DAN.
She died, alack, last sennight.

ST. FRAN.

Did she so ?
If the condolences of men avail
Thee aught, take mine.

DAN.

They are of no avail.

SAV. [*To* LUC.]
I do refuse thee audience.

LUC.

Then why
Didst thou not say so promptly when I ask'd it ?

SAV.
Full well thou knowst that I was interrupted
By Alighieri's entry.

[*Noise without. Enter Guelfs and Ghibellines fighting.*]

What is this ?

Luc.

I did not think that in this cloister'd spot
There would be so much doing. I had look'd
To find Savonarola all alone
And tempt him in his uneventful cell.
Instead o' which—Spurn'd am I ? I am I.
There was a time, Sir, look to 't ! O damnation !
What is 't ? Anon then ! These my toys, my gauds,
That in the cradle—aye, 't my mother's breast—
I puled and lisped at,—'Tis impossible,
Tho', faith, 'tis not so, forasmuch as 'tis.
And I a daughter of the Borgias !—
Or so they told me. Liars ! Flatterers !
Currying lick-spoons ! Where's the Hell of 't then ?
'Tis time that I were going. Farewell, Monk,
But I'll avenge me ere the sun has sunk.

> [*Exeunt* Luc., St. Fran., *and* Leonardo, *followed by* Dan.
> Sav., *having watched* Luc. *out of sight, sinks to his knees,
> sobbing.* Fri. *and* Sacr. *watch him in amazement. Guelfs
> and Ghibellines continue fighting as the Curtain falls.*]

Act II

Time: *Afternoon of same day.*

Scene: *Lucrezia's Laboratory. Retorts, test-tubes, etc. On
small Renaissance table, up* c., *is a great poison-bowl, the
contents of which are being stirred by the* First Apprentice.
The Second Apprentice *stands by, watching him.*

Second App.

For whom is the brew destin'd ?

FIRST APP.

I know not.
Lady Lucrezia did but lay on me
Injunctions as regards the making of 't,
The which I have obey'd. It is compounded
Of a malignant and a deadly weed
Found not save in the Gulf of Spezia,
And one small phial of 't, I am advis'd,
Were more than 'nough to slay a regiment
Of Messer Malatesta's condottieri
In all their armour.

SECOND APP.

I can well believe it.
Mark how the purple bubbles froth upon
The evil surface of its nether slime !

[*Enter* LUC.]

LUC. [*To* FIRST APP.]
Is 't done, Sir Sluggard ?

FIRST APP.

Madam, to a turn.

LUC.
Had it not been so, I with mine own hand
Would have outpour'd it down thy gullet, knave.
See, here's a ring of cunningly-wrought gold
That I, on a dark night, did purchase from
A goldsmith on the Ponte Vecchio.
Small was his shop, and hoar of visage he.
I did bemark that from the ceiling's beams
Spiders had spun their webs for many a year,
The which hung erst like swathes of gossamer

Seen in the shadows of a fairy glade,
But now most woefully were weighted o'er
With gather'd dust. Look well now at the ring!
Touch'd here, behold, it opes a cavity
Capacious of three drops of yon fell stuff.
Dost heed? Whoso then puts it on his finger
Dies, and his soul is from his body rapt
To Hell or Heaven as the case may be.
Take thou this toy and pour the three drops in.

[*Hands ring to* FIRST APP. *and comes down* C.]

So, Sav'narola, thou shalt learn that I
Utter no threats but I do make them good.
Ere this day's sun hath wester'd from the view
Thou art to preach from out the Loggia
Dei Lanzi to the cits in the Piazza.
I, thy Lucrezia, will be upon the steps
To offer thee with phrases seeming-fair
That which shall seal thine eloquence for ever.
O mighty lips that held the world in spell
But would not meet these little lips of mine
In the sweet way that lovers use—O thin,
Cold, tight-drawn, bloodless lips, which natheless I
Deem of all lips the most magnifical
In this our city——

[*Enter the Borgias'* FOOL.]

Well, Fool, what's thy latest?

FOOL

Aristotle's or Zeno's, Lady—'tis neither latest nor last. For, marry,
if the cobbler stuck to his last, then were his latest his last *in
rebus ambulantibus*. Argal, I stick at nothing but cobble-stones,
which, by the same token, are stuck to the road by men's
fingers.

Luc.

How many crows may nest in a grocer's jerkin?

Fool

A full dozen at cock-crow, and something less under the dog-
star, by reason of the dew, which lies heavy on men taken by
the scurvy.

Luc. [*To* First App.]
Methinks the Fool is a fool.

Fool

And therefore, by auricular deduction, am I own twin to the
Lady Lucrezia!

[*Sings.*]

> When pears hang green on the garden wall
> > With a nid, and a nod, and a niddy-niddy-o
> Then prank you, lads and lasses all,
> > With a yea and a nay and a niddy-o.

> But when the thrush flies out o' the frost
> > With a nid, [*etc.*]
> 'Tis time for loons to count the cost,
> > With a yea [*etc.*]

[*Enter the* Porter.]

Porter

O my dear Mistress, there is one below
Demanding to have instant word of thee
I told him that your Ladyship was not
At home. Vain perjury! He would not take
Nay for an answer.

Luc.
Ah ? What manner of man
Is he ?

Porter
A personage the like of whom
Is wholly unfamiliar to my gaze.
Cowl'd is he, but I saw his great eyes glare
From their deep sockets in such wise as leopards
Glare from their caverns, crouching ere they spring
On their reluctant prey.

Luc.
And what name gave he ?

Porter [*After a pause.*]
Something-arola.

Luc.
Savon- ? [Porter nods.] Show him up.

[*Exit* Porter.]
Fool
If he be right astronomically, Mistress, then is he the greater
dunce in respect of true learning, the which goes by the globe.
Argal, 'twere better he widened his wind-pipe.

[*Sings.*]
Fly home, sweet self,
Nothing's for weeping,
Hemp was not made
For lovers' keeping,
Lovers' keeping,
Cheerly, cheerly, fly away.

• 83 •

Hew no more wood
While ash is glowing,
The longest grass
Is lovers' mowing,
Lovers' mowing,
Cheerly, [*etc.*]

[*Re-enter* PORTER, *followed by* SAV. *Exeunt* PORTER, FOOL, *and* FIRST *and* SECOND APPS.]

SAV.

I am no more a monk, I am a man
O' the world.
[*Throws off cowl and frock, and stands forth in the costume of a Renaissance nobleman.* LUCREZIA *looks him up and down.*]

LUC.
Thou cutst a sorry figure.

SAV.
That
Is neither here nor there. I love you, Madam.

LUC.
And this, methinks, is neither there nor here,
For that my love of thee hath vanishèd,
Seeing thee thus beprankt. Go pad thy calves!
Thus mightst thou, just conceivably, with luck
Capture the fancy of some serving-wench.

SAV.
And this is all thou hast to say to me?

Luc.

It is.

Sav.

   I am dismiss'd?

Luc.

                 Thou art.

Sav.

                       'Tis well.

                         [Resumes frock and cowl.]

Savonarola is himself once more.

Luc.

And all my love for him returns to me

A thousandfold !

Sav.

             Too late ! My pride of manhood

Is wounded irremediably. I'll

To the Piazza, where my flock awaits me.

Thus do we see that men make great mistakes

But may amend them when the conscience wakes.

                                [Exit.]

Luc.

I'm half avengèd now, but only half:

'Tis with the ring I'll have the final laugh !

Tho' love be sweet, revenge is sweeter far.

To the Piazza ! Ha, ha, ha, ha, har !

    *[Seizes ring, and exit. Through open door are heard, as
    the Curtain falls, sounds of a terrific hubbub in the Piazza.]*

Act III

Scene: *The Piazza.*

Time: *A few minutes anterior to close of preceding Act.*

The Piazza is filled from end to end with a vast seething crowd that is drawn entirely from the lower orders. There is a sprinkling of wild-eyed and dishevelled women in it. The men are lantern-jawed, with several days' growth of beard. Most of them carry rude weapons—staves, bill-hooks, crow-bars, and the like—and are in as excited a condition as the women. Some are bare-headed, others affect a kind of Phrygian cap. Cobblers predominate.

Enter Lorenzo de Medici and Cosimo de Medici. *They wear cloaks of scarlet brocade, and, to avoid notice, hold masks to their faces.*

Cos.

What purpose doth the foul and greasy plebs
Ensue to-day here?

Lor.

              I nor know nor care.

Cos.

How thrall'd thou art to the philosophy
Of Epicurus! Naught that's human I
Deem alien from myself. [*To a* Cobbler.] Make answer, fellow!
What empty hope hath drawn thee by a thread
Forth from the *obs*cene hovel where thou starvest?

Cob.

No empty hope, your Honour, but the full
Assurance that to-day, as yesterday,
Savonarola will let loose his thunder
Against the vices of the idle rich

And from the brimming cornucopia
Of his immense vocabulary pour
Scorn on the lamentable heresies
Of the New Learning and on all the art
Later than Giotto.

Cos.
                    Mark how absolute
The knave is!

Lor.
                    Then are parrots rational
When they regurgitate the thing they hear!
This fool is but an unit of the crowd,
And crowds are senseless as the vasty deep
That sinks or surges as the moon dictates.
I know these crowds, and know that any man
That hath a glib tongue and a rolling eye
Can as he willeth with them.
        [*Removes his mask and mounts steps of Loggia.*]
                    Citizens!
        [*Prolonged yells and groans from the crowd.*]
Yes, I am he, I am that same Lorenzo
Whom you have nicknamed the Magnificent.
        [*Further terrific yells, shaking of fists, brandishings of bill-
        hooks, insistent cries of 'Death to Lorenzo!' 'Down with the
        Magnificent!' Cobblers on fringe of crowd, down c., ex-
        hibit especially all the symptoms of epilepsy, whooping-
        cough, and other ailments.*]
You love not me.
        [*The crowd makes an ugly rush. Lor. appears likely to
        be dragged down and torn limb from limb, but raises one
        hand in nick of time, and continues:*]
                    Yet I deserve your love.

[*The yells are now variegated with dubious murmurs. A cobbler down* c. *thrusts his face feverishly in the face of another and repeats, in a hoarse interrogative whisper, 'Deserves our love?'*]

Not for the sundry boons I have bestow'd
And benefactions I have lavishèd
Upon Firenze, City of the Flowers,
But for the love that in this rugged breast
I bear you.

[*The yells have now died away, and there is a sharp fall in dubious murmurs. The cobbler down* c. *says, in an ear-piercing whisper, 'The love he bears us,' drops his lower jaw, nods his head repeatedly, and awaits in an intolerable state of suspense the orator's next words.*]

      I am not a blameless man,

[*Some dubious murmurs.*]

Yet for that I have lov'd you passing much,
Shall some things be forgiven me.

[*Noises of cordial assent.*]

      There dwells
In this our city, known unto you all,
A man more virtuous than I am, and
A thousand times more intellectual;
Yet envy not I him, for—shall I name him?—
He loves not you. His name? I will not cut
Your hearts by speaking it. Here let it stay
On tip o' tongue.

[*Insistent clamour.*]

      Then steel you to the shock!—
Savonarola.

[*For a moment or so the crowd reels silently under the shock. Cobbler down* c. *is the first to recover himself and*

cry 'Death to Savonarola!' The cry instantly becomes
general. LOR. holds up his hand and gradually imposes
silence.]

    His twin bug-bears are
Yourselves and that New Learning which I hold
Less dear than only you.

[*Profound sensation. Everybody whispers 'Than only you'
to everybody else. A woman near steps of Loggia attempts
to kiss hem of* LOR.'s *garment.*]

      Would you but con
With me the old philosophers of Hellas,
Her fervent bards and calm historians,
You would arise and say 'We will not hear
Another word against them!'

[*The crowd already says this, repeatedly, with great em-
phasis.*]

      Take the Dialogues
Of Plato, for example. You will find
A spirit far more truly Christian
In them than in the ravings of the sour-soul'd
Savonarola.

[*Prolonged cries of 'Death to the Sour-Souled Savonarola!'
Several cobblers detach themselves from the crowd and
rush away to read the Platonic Dialogues. Enter* SAVONAROLA.
*The crowd, as he makes his way through it, gives up all
further control of its feelings, and makes a noise for which
even the best zoologists might not find a good comparison.
The staves and bill-hooks wave like twigs in a storm. One
would say that* SAV. *must have died a thousand deaths already. He is, however, unharmed and unruffled as he
reaches the upper step of the Loggia.* LOR. *meanwhile
has rejoined* COS. *in the Piazza.*]

SAV.

>   Pax vobiscum, brothers !

> [*This does but exacerbate the crowd's frenzy.*]

VOICE OF A COBBLER

Hear his false lips cry Peace when there is no
Peace !

SAV.

>   Are not you ashamed, O Florentines,

> [*Renewed yells, but also some symptoms of manly shame.*]

That hearken'd to Lorenzo and now reel
Inebriate with the exuberance
Of his verbosity ?

> [*The crowd makes an obvious effort to pull itself together.*]

>   A man can fool

Some of the people all the time, and can
Fool all the people sometimes, but he cannot
Fool *all* the people *all* the time.

> [*Loud cheers. Several cobblers clap one another on the back. Cries of 'Death to Lorenzo !' The meeting is now well in hand.*]

>   To-day

I must adopt a somewhat novel course
In dealing with the awful wickedness
At present noticeable in this city.
I do so with reluctance. Hitherto
I have avoided personalities.
But now my sense of duty forces me
To a departure from my custom of
Naming no names. One name I must and shall
Name.

[*All eyes are turned on* LOR., *who smiles uncomfortably.*]
    No, I do not mean Lorenzo. He
Is 'neath contempt.

[*Loud and prolonged laughter, accompanied with hideous
grimaces at* LOR. *Exeunt* LOR. *and* COS.]
                I name a woman's name,

[*The women in the crowd eye one another suspiciously.*]
A name known to you all—four-syllablèd,
Beginning with an L.

[*Tense pause. Enter* LUC., *carrying the ring, and stands, un-
observed by any one, on outskirt of crowd.* SAV. *utters the
name:*]
                Lucrezia !

LUC. [*With equal intensity.*]
Savonarola !

[SAV. *starts violently and stares in direction of her voice.*]
           Yes, I come, I come !

[*Forces her way to steps of Loggia. The crowd is much be-
wildered, and the cries of 'Death to Lucrezia Borgia!' are
few and sporadic.*]
Why didst thou call me ?

                [SAV. *looks somewhat embarrassed.*]
                What is thy distress ?
I see it all ! The sanguinary mob
Clusters to rend thee ! As the antler'd stag,
With fine eyes glazèd from the too-long chase,
Turns to defy the foam-fleck'd pack, and thinks,
In his last moment, of some graceful hind
Seen once afar upon a mountain-top,
E'en so, Savonarola, didst thou think,

H   · 91 ·

In thy most dire extremity, of me.
And here I am ! Courage ! The horrid hounds
Droop tail at sight of me and fawn away
Innocuous.

[*The crowd does indeed seem to have fallen completely under the sway of* Luc.*'s magnetism, and is evidently convinced that it had been about to make an end of the monk.*]

Take thou, and wear henceforth,
As a sure talisman 'gainst future perils,
This little, little ring.

[Sav. *makes awkward gesture of refusal. Angry murmurs from the crowd. Cries of 'Take thou the ring !' 'Churl !' 'Put it on !' etc.*

Enter the Borgias' Fool *and stands unnoticed on fringe of crowd.*]

I hoped you 'ld like it—
Neat but not gaudy. Is my taste at fault ?
I'd so look'd forward to— [*Sob.*] No, I'm not crying,
But just a little hurt.

[*Hardly a dry eye in the crowd. Also swayings and snarlings indicative that* Sav.*'s life is again not worth a moment's purchase.* Sav. *makes awkward gesture of acceptance, but just as he is about to put ring on finger, the* Fool *touches his lute and sings:—*]

Wear not the ring,
It hath an unkind sting,
Ding, dong, ding.

Bide a minute,
There's poison in it,
Poison in it,

Ding-a-dong, dong, ding.

Luc.

The fellow lies.

[*The crowd is torn with conflicting opinions. Mingled cries of 'Wear not the ring!' 'The fellow lies!' 'Bide a minute!' 'Death to the Fool!' 'Silence for the Fool!' 'Ding-a-dong, dong, ding!' etc.*]

FOOL

[*Sings.*]

Wear not the ring,
For Death's a robber-king,
     Ding, [*etc.*]

There's no trinket
Is what you think it,
     What you think it,
          Ding-a-dong, [*etc.*]

[Sav. *throws ring in* Luc.'s *face. Enter* POPE JULIUS II, *with Papal army.*]

POPE

Arrest that man and woman!

[*Re-enter Guelfs and Ghibellines fighting.* Sav. *and* Luc. *are arrested by Papal officers. Enter* MICHAEL ANGELO. ANDREA DEL SARTO *appears for a moment at a window.* PIPPA *passes. Brothers of the Misericordia go by, singing a Requiem for Francesca da Rimini. Enter* BOCCACCIO, BENVENUTO CELLINI, *and many others, making remarks highly characteristic of themselves but scarcely audible through the terrific thunderstorm which now bursts over Florence and is at its loudest and darkest crisis as the Curtain falls.*]

Act IV

Time: *Three hours later.*

Scene: *A Dungeon on the ground-floor of the Palazzo Civico.*
The stage is bisected from top to bottom by a wall, on one side of which is seen the interior of Lucrezia's *cell, on the other that of* Savonarola's.

Neither he nor she knows that the other is in the next cell. The audience, however, knows this.

Each cell (because of the width and height of the proscenium) is of more than the average Florentine size, but is bare even to the point of severity, its sole amenities being some straw, a hunk of bread, and a stone pitcher. The door of each is facing the audience. Dim-ish light.

Lucrezia *wears long and clanking chains on her wrists, as does also* Savonarola. *Imprisonment has left its mark on both of them.* Savonarola's *hair has turned white. His whole aspect is that of a very old, old man.* Lucrezia *looks no older than before, but has gone mad.*

Sav.

Alas, how long ago this morning seems
This evening ! A thousand thousand æons
Are scarce the measure of the gulf betwixt
My then and now. Methinks I must have been
Here since the dim creation of the world
And never in that interval have seen
The tremulous hawthorn burgeon in the brake,
Nor heard the hum o' bees, nor woven chains
Of buttercups on Mount Fiesole
What time the sap lept in the cypresses,
Imbuing with the friskfulness of Spring
Those melancholy trees. I do forget
The aspect of the sun. Yet I was born

A freeman, and the Saints of Heaven smiled
Down on my crib. What would my sire have said,
And what my dam, had anybody told them
The time would come when I should occupy
A felon's cell? O the disgrace of it! —
The scandal, the incredible come-down!
It masters me. I see i' my mind's eye
The public prints—'Sharp Sentence on a Monk.'
What then? I thought I was of sterner stuff
Than is affrighted by what people think.
Yet thought I so because 'twas thought of me,
And so 'twas thought of me because I had
A hawk-like profile and a baleful eye.
Lo! my soul's chin recedes, soft to the touch
As half-churn'd butter. Seeming hawk is dove,
And dove's a gaol-bird now. Fie, out upon 't!

Luc.

How comes it? I am Empress Dowager
Of China—yet was never crown'd. This must
Be seen to.

> [*Quickly gathers some straw and weaves a crown, which she puts on.*]

Sav.

       O, what a dégringolade!
The great career I had mapp'd out for me—
Nipp'd i' the bud. What life, when I come out,
Awaits me? Why, the very Novices
And callow Postulants will draw aside
As I pass by, and say 'That man hath done
Time!' And yet shall I wince? The worst of Time
Is not in having done it, but in doing 't.

LUC.

Ha, ha, ha, ha! Eleven billion pig-tails
Do tremble at my nod imperial,—
The which is as it should be.

SAV.

                                    I have heard
That gaolers oft are willing to carouse
With them they watch o'er, and do sink at last
Into a drunken sleep, and then's the time
To snatch the keys and make a bid for freedom.
Gaoler! Ho, Gaoler!

> [*Sounds of lock being turned and bolts withdrawn. Enter
> the Borgias'* FOOL, *in plain clothes, carrying bunch of
> keys.*]
                                    I have seen thy face
Before.

FOOL

        I saved thy life this afternoon, Sir.

SAV.

Thou art the Borgias' Fool?

FOOL

                              Say rather, was.
Unfortunately I have been discharg'd
For my betrayal of Lucrezia,
So that I have to speak like other men—
Decasyllabically, and with sense.
An hour ago the gaoler of this dungeon
Died of an apoplexy. Hearing which,
I ask'd for and obtain'd his billet.

Sav.

Fetch
A stoup o' liquor for thyself and me.

[*Exit* Gaoler.]

Freedom ! there's nothing that thy votaries
Grudge in the cause of thee. That decent man
Is doom'd by me to lose his place again
To-morrow morning when he wakes from out
His hoggish slumber. Yet I care not.

[*Re-enter* Gaoler *with a leathern bottle and two glasses.*]

Ho !
This is the stuff to warm our vitals, this
The panacea for all mortal ills
And sure elixir of eternal youth.
Drink, bonniman !

[Gaoler *drains a glass and shows signs of instant intoxica-
tion.* Sav. *claps him on shoulder and replenishes glass.*
Gaoler *drinks again, lies down on floor, and snores.* Sav.
*snatches the bunch of keys, laughs long but silently, and
creeps out on tip-toe, leaving door ajar.*

Luc. *meanwhile has lain down on the straw in her cell,
and fallen asleep.*

*Noise of bolts being shot back, jangling of keys, grating
of lock, and the door of* Luc.'s *cell flies open.* Sav. *takes
two steps across the threshold, his arms outstretched and his
upturned face transfigured with a great joy.*]

How sweet the open air
Leaps to my nostrils ! O the good brown earth
That yields once more to my elastic tread
And laves these feet with its remember'd dew !

[*Takes a few more steps, still looking upwards.*]

Free ! I am free ! O naked arc of heaven,

Enspangled with innumerable—no,
Stars are not there. Yet neither are there clouds !
The thing looks like a ceiling ! [*Gazes downward.*] And
    this thing
Looks like a floor. [*Gazes around.*] And that white
    bundle yonder
Looks curiously like Lucrezia.

    [Luc. *awakes at sound of her name, and sits up sane.*]

There must be some mistake.

Luc. [*Rises to her feet.*]

                 There is indeed !
A pretty sort of prison I have come to,
In which a self-respecting lady's cell
Is treated as a lounge !

Sav.

             I had no notion
You were in here. I thought I was out there.
I will explain—but first I'll make amends.
Here are the keys by which your durance ends.
The gate is somewhere in this corridor,
And so good-bye to this interior !

    [*Exeunt* Sav. *and* Luc. *Noise, a moment later, of a key
    grating in a lock, then of gate creaking on its hinges;
    triumphant laughs of fugitives; loud slamming of gate be-
    hind them.*

      In Sav.'s *cell the* Gaoler *starts in his sleep, turns his
    face to the wall, and snores more than ever deeply. Through
    open door comes a cloaked figure.*]

Cloaked Figure
Sleep on, Savonarola, and awake

Not in this dungeon but in ruby Hell !

[*Stabs* GAOLER, *whose snores cease abruptly. Enter* POPE
JULIUS II, *with Papal retinue carrying torches.* MURDERER
steps quickly back into shadow.]

POPE [*To body of* GAOLER.]
Savonarola, I am come to taunt
Thee in thy misery and dire abjection.
Rise, Sir, and hear me out.

MURD. [*Steps forward.*]
                              Great Julius,
Waste not thy breath. Savonarola's dead.
I murder'd him.

POPE
                    Thou hadst no right to do so.
Who art thou, pray ?

MURD.
                    Cesare Borgia,
Lucrezia's brother, and I claim a brother's
Right to assassinate whatever man
Shall wantonly and in cold blood reject
Her timid offer of a poison'd ring.

POPE
Of this anon.
                              [*Stands over body of* GAOLER.]
            Our present business
Is general woe. No nobler corse hath ever
Impress'd the ground. O, let the trumpets speak it !
                              [*Flourish of trumpets.*]
This was the noblest of the Florentines.

His character was flawless, and the world
Held not his parallel. O, bear him hence
With all such honours as our State can offer.
He shall interrèd be with noise of cannon,
As doth befit so militant a nature.
Prepare these obsequies.

> [*Papal officers lift body of* GAOLER.]

A PAPAL OFFICER

                But this is not
Savonarola. It is some one else.

CESARE

Lo! 'tis none other than the Fool that I
Hoof'd from my household but two hours agone.
I deem'd him no good riddance, for he had
The knack of setting tables on a roar.
What shadows we pursue! Good night, sweet Fool,
And flights of angels sing thee to thy rest!

POPE

Interrèd shall he be with signal pomp.
No honour is too great that we can pay him.
He leaves the world a vacuum. Meanwhile,
Go we in chase of the accursèd villain
That hath made escapado from this cell.
To horse! Away! We'll scour the country round
For Sav'narola till we hold him bound.
Then shall you see a cinder, not a man,
Beneath the lightnings of the Vatican!

> [*Flourish, alarums and excursions, flashes of Vatican light-*
> *ning, roll of drums, etc. Through open door of cell is led*
> *in a large milk-white horse, which the* POPE *mounts as the*
> *Curtain falls.*]

Act V (Scenario)

Dawn on summit of Mount Fiesole. Outspread view of Florence (Duomo, Giotto's Tower, etc.) as seen from that eminence.—Niccolo Machiavelli, *asleep on grass, wakes as sun rises. Deplores his exile from Florence,* Lorenzo's *unappeasable hostility, etc. Wonders if he could not somehow secure the* Pope's *favour. Very cynical. Breaks off*: But who are these that scale the mountain-side? | Savonarola and Lucrezia | Borgia! —*Enter through a trap-door, back* c. [*trap-door veiled from audience by a grassy ridge*], Sav. *and* Luc. *Both gasping and footsore from their climb.* [*Still with chains on their wrists? or not?*]— Mach. *steps unobserved behind a cypress and listens.* —Sav. *has a speech to the rising sun*—Th' effulgent hope that westers from the east | Daily. *Says that his hope, on the contrary, lies in escape* To that which easters not from out the west, | That fix'd abode of freedom which men call | America! *Very bitter against* Pope.—Luc. *says that she, for her part, means* To start afresh in that uncharted land | Which austers not from out the antipod, | Australia!—*Exit* Mach., *unobserved, down trap-door behind ridge, to betray* Luc. *and* Sav.—*Several longish speeches by* Sav. *and* Luc. *Time is thus given for* Mach. *to get into touch with* Pope, *and time for* Pope *and retinue to reach the slope of Fiesole.* Sav., *glancing down across ridge, sees these sleuth-hounds, points them out to* Luc. *and cries* Bewray'd! Luc. By whom? Sav. I know not, but suspect | The hand of that sleek serpent Niccolo | Machiavelli.—Sav. *and* Luc. *rush down* c., *but find their way barred by the footlights.*—Luc. We will not be ta'en | Alive. And here availeth us my lore | In what pertains to poison. Yonder herb | [*points to a herb growing down* R.] Is deadly nightshade. Quick, Monk! Pluck we it!—*Sav. and* Luc. *die just as* POPE *appears over ridge, followed by retinue in full cry.— POPE's annoyance at being foiled is quickly swept away on the great wave of Shakespearean chivalry and charity that again rises in him. He gives* SAV. *a funeral oration similar to the one meant for him in Act IV, but even more laudatory and more stricken. Of* LUC., *too, he enumerates the virtues, and hints that the whole terrestrial globe shall be hollowed to receive her bones. Ends by saying:* In deference to this our double sorrow | Sun shall not shine to-day nor shine to-morrow.—*Sun drops quickly back behind eastern horizon, leaving a great darkness on which the Curtain slowly falls.*

§ 60

Ballad of a recurring anomaly
in Berkeley Square

O, Berkeley Square is brown and green,
 With its ancient bricks and grass,
There's never a lad can tell how old
 'Twill be come Candlemas.

Its hoary pride holds even now
 Democracy at bay,
And revels in gaunt memories
 Of George the Third his day.

O, good to see on either side
 Of some great Noble's porch
An iron-wrought extinguisher
 For the running footman's torch,

And good to see that when she fares
 Forth to some rout or ball
His Lady has a stepping-stone
 To mount her coach withal!

Stands that great landmark, Lansdowne House—
 O, stands it where it did?
Yea, as irrefragably as
 Cheops his pyramid.

And round the Square's three other sides
 Old Tories and old Whigs
Splendidly, crabbedly defy
 Time and his whirligigs.

Yet, ever since my childhood's hour
    (And that is now remote)
I've found in this harmonious Square
    One slightly jarring note.

I think it was in 'eighty-three,
    Or praps a trifle later,
That Mr. Bancroft came here from
    The Haymarket Theayter,

And with him his good lady—whose
    Goodness, I grieve to state,
Was commonly regarded as
    A thing of recent date.

They came, these two. The grim façades
    Seemed to frown black with thunder
Olympian (and I am bound
    To say I didn't wonder).

But, as time passed, this frown relaxed,
    By reason that this pair
Were so pathetically keen
    To live up to this Square.

Bancroft himself tried hard to look
    Not like a bold bad mime,
But like a fine old English Gentleman—
    One of the Olden Time.

And not less hard his lady strove
    To compass the effect
Of a firmly-based Victorian dame—
    One of the straitest sect.

Gallant Val Baker she lived down,
    And down Alf Edinborough.
Mother and wife, she had but one
    Word for her motto: Thorough.

And yet, however earnestly
    The Bancroft couple strove,
Always I wished them somewhere else—
    Somewhere in Westbourne Grove.

It seemed to my old-fashioned sense
    That they, for all their care,
Misfitted the amenities
    Of Berkeley's holy Square.

The years rolled by. From out his home
    Bancroft, in chaste apparel,
Went reading to the Provinces
    Dickens's Christmas Carol.

It mastered him, that simple tale,
    It emptied him of pride,
It set him longing for some in-
    conspicuous fireside—

A small hearth in an humble cot,
    Hid far from Mammon's eye. . . .
Sir Squire and Lady Bancroft moved
    Into the Albany.

'Now Heaven be praised!' said I. 'Henceforth'—
    But that is all I said.
Lo, Seymour Hickses had rushed in
    Where Bancrofts ceased to tread.

Perspiring Seymour suddenly
    Had darted on the scene,
With that sweet old English rosebud,
    The winsome Ellaline.

I said, 'In this Square's atmosphere
    You're both of you all wrong !'
'Oh, surely not !' said Ellaline;
    Said Seymour, 'Go along !'

For a brief, brief while they revelled here,
    Cutting a great, great dash;
Then, in the street called Portugal,
    I heard a deaf-ning crash:

Hicks had gone broke. He swam away
    In floods of perspiration,
Which must have added greatly to
    That other liquidation.

'Now Heaven be praised !' said I. 'Henceforth'—
    But the words died on my lips. . . .
Behold, two scorpions came to take
    The place of those two whips.

A svelte young person, whose good name
    Was wholly without voucher,
Came languishing upon the arm
    Of Mr. Rarthur Bourchier.

Rarthur, it seems, had recently
    Writ in his mad agenda:
'Commodious Mansion—Berkeley Square—
    Miss Bellew—Guilty Splenda !'

So here they were—yea, and still are.
    Throughout the stricken Square
The grass lies withered, and the trees
    Stand blasted, writhen, bare.

You think that I exaggerate?
    I daresay that I do.
Had you loved this Square as much as I
    Have loved it, so would you.

No!—do not try to comfort me!
    Rarthur will hook it soon?
Yes, yes, his gun is even now
    Aimed straight up at the moon.

But after that,—what then, what next?
    Something, I feel, still worse,
Will settle down upon the Square,
    To carry on the curse.

I feel that one of these august
    Houses (I'm not sure which)
Is destined to contain the vast
    Harem of Little Tich.

Rapallo and Abinger
1919 and After

§ 61

After Tom Moore

When the white rose of theft and the red rose of arson
Shall fade in the gardens they bloom in to-day,
The sun will avail not to wither the grass on
The grave of the lovely Amanda O'Shea!

Her eyes were so blue and her lips were so trustful,
And her heart was so like to the heart of a dove,
That men in her presence were pure and not lustful
And kissed but the kid of her lily-white glove.

She was fairest of all the fair daughters of Erin,
With the grace that the maids of Circassia possess;
And her eye there was always a spark or a tear in—
A spark of amusement, a tear of distress.

She sat on a rout-seat when first I espied her,
The lights of the ballroom less bright than her brow,
And I thought not of Time, the relentless divider:
She lies in the vault of her ancestors now.

Were ever such bandeaux of raven-black tresses
As framed so divinely that oval, her face?
She wore the most perfect of evening dresses
A dream of white satin—a triumph of grace!

That satin, alas, now is sere and is yellow,
The grave that she lies in is dark as her hair;
Tho' years have evanished, there's naught can make mellow
The sorrow I feel and the grief that I bear.

· 111 ·

No matter !—I'll see her, an angel with pinions
As white as the robe that she wore at the ball,
On a seat of pure gold in celestial dominions—
The fairest of any, the blandest of all !

§ 62

In Max's copy of Housman's
A Shropshire Lad

And now, lad, all is over
'Twixt you, your love, and the clover;
    So keep a stiff upper-lip
And shrink not, lad, nor shiver,
But walk you down to the river
    And take your final dip.
           Vide hunc libellum passim

§ 63. A poem John Galsworthy inscribed in the autograph-cum-guest book kept by Sir Edward Marsh inspired Max, on the page following, to contribute:

A Prayer

If I popped in at Downing Street
And Eddie were at home,
What is the pome wherewith I'd greet
Him ? I will write the pome:

    'O, Eddie, dear old boy,
    O, C.M.G., C.B.,
    Make firm in me a heart too coy
    To write a pome for thee !'

§ 64. As in his earlier 'Elegy on Any Lady,' Max was amused by George Moore's desire to be regarded as a lady-killer.

Vague Lyric by G. M.

I met Musette
In the water-closet—
Or if it wasn't there, where *was* it?
And let me see:
Was it not Mimi
That made such passionate love to me
In the W.C.?
Which *was* it?

§ 65

In a copy of W. J. Turner's *Paris and Helen*

O glen, grove, dale, vale, glade, grove, glen,
    Right good are ye to dwell in;
But when is Paris coming—when?
    And where the Hell is Helen?

§ 66

To H. G.-B.

The Theatre's in a parlous state,
    I readily admit;
It almost is exanimate—
    But then, when *wasn't* it ?
It always *was, will* always be;
    God has decreed it so.
Can'st thou rescind His grim decree ?
    O, my dear Harley, No !

In Shakespeare's and in Marlowe's day,*
    In Congreve's, in Racine's,
The wretched Theatre murmured 'I'm
    One of the Might-Have-Beens !'
'O May-Be-Yet !' the critics cried,
    '*We*'ll teach you how to grow !'
And were their fond hopes gratified ?
    O, my dear Harley, No !

The Theatre is Exemplary,
    Now as in other ages,
Of all a Theatre shouldn't be—
    Of all that most enrages
Right-thinking men like you and me
    And plunges us in woe . . .
Mightn't perhaps the L.C.C.——
    O, my dear Harley, No !

Shall cubits come by taking thought,
　　And Drama gain her soul
By learning what she doubtless ought
　　From dear old Mr. Poel?
Shall syllabi and seminars
　　And blackboards all in a row
Somehow uplift us to the stars?
　　O, my dear Harley, No!

*I meant to write in my MS
　　'Time'—and wrote 'day,' it seems.
This error fills me with distress
　　And haunts me in my dreams.
A lover I'm of chime of rhyme,
　　And to *vers libres* a foe . . .
Shall such a man rhyme 'day' with 'I'm'?
　　O, my dear Harley, No!

§ 67

Sir Herbert Vansittart

Ah, did you once see Prinny plain,
　　And did he stop and speak to you
And did you speak to him again?
　　How strange it seems, and new!

§ 68

Triolets

composed on a day when I thought

(from what he had said on a previous day)

that Harley wouldn't turn up for luncheon

Harley's doing Cymbeline;
    Helen takes a car.
Behind yon castellated screen
Harley's doing Cymbeline.
Beetle-browed, athletic, lean,
    Aloof, alone, afar,
Harley's doing Cymbeline . . .
    Helen takes a car.

Helen eats and drinks with us;
    Harley plies his quill.
Gracious, fair, diaphanous
Helen eats and drinks with us . . .
Utterly oblivious
    Of Stratford's clever Will,
Helen eats and drinks with us;
    Harley plies his quill.

Helen's way is right;
　　Harley's way is wrong.
As 'twere a swallow's flight,
Helen's way is right,—
To flit, to swoop, to alight
　　And gladden us with song !
Helen's way is right.
　　Harley's way is wrong.

(Supplementary triolet, composed at luncheon.)

Oh, bother and damn !
　　These verses won't do !
How unlucky I am !
Oh, bother and damn !
Harley, that sham,
　　Has alighted here too !
Oh, bother and damn !
　　These verses won't do !

PS. Feb. 27.

Still, here they are,
　　With my love to you both.
From perfect they're far,—
Still, here they are.
They're away below par,
　　And to *write* them I'm loth.
Still, here they are,
　　With my love to you both.

§ 69

A Luncheon

Lift latch, step in, be welcome, Sir,
Albeit to see you I'm unglad
And your face is fraught with a deathly shyness
Bleaching what pink it may have had.
Come in, come in, Your Royal Highness.

Beautiful weather ?—Sir, that's true,
Though the farmers are casting rueful looks
At tilth's and pasture's dearth of spryness.—
Yes, Sir, I've written several books.—
A little more chicken, Your Royal Highness ?

Lift latch, step out, your car is there,
To bear you hence from this antient vale.
We are both of us aged by our strange brief nighness,
But each of us lives to tell the tale.
Farewell, farewell, Your Royal Highness.

§ 70.   It is impossible to place this poem in the sequence of Soames's work, beyond assuming that it was written after the autumn of '96—when his last volume appeared (published at his own expense)—and of course before the tragic events of the 3rd of June 1897. Too, it is more sustained than his verses from *Fungoids*, presented earlier as 35 and 36.

Tracked

Enoch Soames

An unpublished sonnet by Enoch Soames

(Communicated by Max Beerbohm)

He raked the ashes from the rusty grate,
Coaxed the dull embers to a tremulous flame,
And laid thereon the ashes of his shame.
They burned in wreaths and spirals delicate,
They vanished. That was done at any rate.
Still, 'twixt the curtain and the window-frame,
Lurked that soft other thing of evil name
Which was less easy to annihilate.
And what if—— Hark ! He stood erect and still.
Then tip-toed noiselessly across the floor
And listened. What if long-lipped Radziwill
Knew ? He knelt down, a man most loth to die,
And, peering through the key-hole of the door,
Saw there the pupil of another eye.

§ 71

In Max's copy of
Ianthe Dunbar's *The Edge of the Desert*

True to your pledge
        You haven't gone far . . .
Is it even the *Edge*,
        Ianthe Dunbar ?

§ 72

Ballade of an Old Fogey

I'm still elastic. I have often thought
        The charm of Bridge superior to Whist's.
Nothing because it's new I set at naught.
        But oh these tale-despising novelists
        And play-eliminating dramatists—
I find it hard to grasp what they are at . . .
        Art's not their game ? They are Evangelists ? . . .
I must confess I don't quite follow that.

I used to haunt the studios and fought
        For Manet's sunshine and for Whistler's mists
And all that Corot had divinely wrought.
        But now I'm told the Post-Impressionists
        And still more recently the Futurists
Have knocked those masters into a cocked-hat,
        And even A. E. John no more exists . . .
I must confess I don't quite follow that.

I seek the Grail that I have always sought.
    Yea ! though I dote, the old young zeal persists:
I still dine out to learn what may be taught,
      But when great dames, with diamonded wrists
      And ears and breasts, say they are Socialists
Biding a flood in which no Ararat
      Will be reserved for the capitalists,
I must confess I don't quite follow that.

ENVOI

England ! I love you and your Colonists,
But Mr. Kipling, throwing up his hat,
Says only cads may be Imperialists . . .
I must confess I don't quite follow that.

§ 73

On Proust

Dear Esther S.——I'm in distress,
It's very sad! My taste is bad.
The men that boost the work of Proust
(Those scholars and those Gentlemen,
Those erudite and splendid men,
Of whom the chief is Scott Moncrieff)
All leave me cold. Perhaps I'm old?
'The reason why, I cannot tell,
I do not like thee, Doctor Fell. . . .'
But *why* not like the late Marcel? . . .
Perhaps he wrote not very well?
This, *bien entendu*, cannot be
He was a Prince of Paragons
(As undergraduates all agree—
Or did in nineteen-twenty-three—
With full concurrence of the Dons).
I only know that all his Swanns
Are now, as ever, geese to me.
Pity the blindness of poor M. B.!
P.S. How sad that I'm alive!
October Nineteen-twenty-five.

§ 74

Sonnet to the
'Most Distinguished Chancellor'
that Oxford Has Had

Curzon ! thou shouldst be living at this hour;
Harold hath need of thee; the Viscount Cave,
Plodding through parchments down into the grave,
Takes not his fancy, and he sees thee tower
High o'er that dallier in Amanda's bower,
The so-called Iron Duke; we hear him rave
Against the folly that to Oxford gave
A sad old Cecil's presence for her dower.
Thy soul was like a Star, and like a Garter;
Thy brow was as a great calm Eagle's egg,
And, like Sir Willoughby, thou hadst a leg;
So didst thou awe earth, sky, clouds, azure main;
And Harold would incontinently barter
His pure young soul to see thee rise again.

§ 75

On Sir Alfred Mond

Plainness, my dear old Alfred Mond,
Is doubtless a solemn and sacred bond;
But surely there must be precious few
Thousands of people as plain as you ?

§ 76

In the Store-Room at King's Land

Some seventy volumes, shelf upon shelf,
All of them written by Belloc himself.
    O fruitful vine! And, down below,
    Seventy dozen bottles or so
Fulfill'd with vintages old and fine
    In love of which I yield to none.
But that august array of wine
Was muster'd from many and many a vine.
    Pour me the fruit of the single one!

§ 77

Epitaph for G. B. Shaw

I strove with all, for all were worth my strife.
    Nature I loathed, and, next to Nature, Art.
I chilled both feet on the thin ice of Life.
    It broke, and I emit one final fart.

§ 78

The Road to Zoagli

(Ligurian Folk Song)

[saved at the last moment by Cecil Max Beerbohm Sharp]

Have ye seen the would-be-not-humble dandy,
    With his long black cloak and his short trousers grey?
I saw him, dear heart, this morn as ever was, on the
                          road to Zoagli,
    And I looked the other way.

What said the would-be-not-humble dandy,
    With his long black cloak and his short trousers grey?
He said naught, dear heart, this morn as ever was, on the
                          road to Zoagli,
    And I looked the other way.

How fared the would-be-not-humble dandy,
    With his long black cloak and his short trousers grey?
He fared ill, dear heart, this morn as ever was, on the
                          road to Zoagli,
    For dead he lay.

§ 79

After Kipling's 'Recessional'

Fred Whyte, 'e done me bloody proud,
So to Je'ovah Thunder-Browed
Says I, 'O Jah, be with me yet,
Lest I forget, lest I forget.'

§ 80

To the Editor of *The Isis*

Believe me, Sir, your undersigned
Servant would gladly turn his mind
From the Universal Crisis
By writing something for THE ISIS—
Something of a sprightly kind
Worthy of the dear old ISIS
(England's best-edited weekly paper);
But things have come to such a pass
Of awful Chaos that, alas,
I cannot cut a single caper—
Nor even find a rhyme to Beerbohm.
Yours obediently,
                              Max Beerbohm.

§ 81

Addition to Kipling's
'The Dead King (Edward VII.), 1910'

Wisely and well was it said of him, 'Hang it all, he's a
Mixture of Jesus, Apollo, Goliath and Julius Caesar !'
Always he plans as an ever Do-Right-man, never an Err-man,
And never a drop of the blood in his beautiful body was German.
'God save him,' we said when he lived, but the words now
                                                    sound odd,
For we know that in Heaven above at this moment *he's* saving
                                                    God.

§ 82

Old Surrey Saws and Sayings

Collected and communicated by Sir Max Beerbohm, P.R.A.

(Professor of Rural Archaeology)

It isn't the singing kettle that scalds the cook's hand.

Snow in January, woe in February.

A word from the Parson is worth a screed from the Squire.

It's poor grass that cannot be cropped under a waning moon.

> A red sky at night
> Is a shepherd's delight,
> A red sky in the morning
> Is a shepherd's warning,
> A sky that looks bad
> Is a shepherd's plaid,
> A good-looking sky
> Is a shepherd's pie.

Better a mouthful at dawn than a bellyful at sunset.

There's many a catch
'Twixt Hammer and Hatch.

Light i' the head, strong i' the arm.

He that hath no teeth hath no toothache.

Bookham for thinking, Stonebridge for doing, Dorking for talking.

A dumb woman sees more things than a blind man hears.

What hasn't been lost can't be found.

Don't beat the bounds before you've baked the apples.

There's never a dam without a sire.

Hounds turn tail when a mad bull gores the running fox.

What Abinger thinks to-day, Dorking will think to-morrow.

§ 83

February 14th 1945

Several Bishops Valentine
with different powers of blessing
give me courage where I stand
with a garland in my hand
partiality confessing
in a tender line.

Saints of Smyrna, France and Crete,
(in whose service I have made
many sonnets and such rhymes
for different loves at different times
as we dallied in the shade,
or they languished at my feet,)

stand beside me as I say,
on their festival and day,
'Sir Max, please be my Valentine
and keep this nonsense, which is mine.'

§ 84. This snook cocked at punditry is the latest-known rhyme of sixty-
two years of Max in verse.

To Dr. D.

Honoured Doctor Dryasdust,
Look to your laurels: you really *must*.
You seem so very moist indeed
When one compares you with Herbert Read.

SOURCES and ANNOTATIONS

§ 1. *Carmen Becceriense*

Printed from the copy of the first edition in Charterhouse School Library, by courtesy of ·Mr. C. F. H. Evans, M.A., F.S.A., Librarian of Charterhouse, Godalming, Surrey.

Composed July 1890. Mr. A. H. Tod, then a master at Charterhouse, had twenty-five copies printed by a Godalming printer, presumably Messrs, R. B. Stedman, who printed the school periodical *The Carthusian* at that time. The copy in Charterhouse School Library is on yellow paper; it bears neither the date of publication nor the name of the printer or publisher.

"Carmen Becceriense" was reprinted in *The Carthusian*, X (April 1912), p. 574. *See* Charles Evans, "A Note on 'Carmen Becceriense'," *The Book Collector*, I (Winter 1952), pp. 215-218, which contains a photographic reproduction of the first edition of the poem. Charterhouse School Library also possesses the manuscript, which differs slightly from the printed version.

The subject of these verses, Arthur G. Becker, was Max's music-master at Charterhouse, and taught the piano. The reference in line 9 is to George Henry Robinson, another music teacher at Charterhouse, and House Master of Robinites, Max's first boardinghouse.

In his various notes Max refers to such classical scholars as John Eyton Bickersteth Mayor (1825-1910), Johan Nicolai Madvig (1804-1886), John Conington (1825-1869), and Karl Gottlob Zumpt (1792-1894). "Mr. T. E. Page": Thomas Ethelbert Page (1850-?), a master at Charterhouse and author of school editions of works of Horace and Virgil. That he was Max's Latin teacher may be inferred from the title page of the 1898 edition of his *Horatii Opera* (first edition, 1883), where he is identified as "T. E. Page, M.A., late Fellow of St. John's College, Cambridge; Assistant Master at Charterhouse," and the Preface, signed, and dated "Charterhouse, Godalming, September 1895." Page's Preface to his *Bucolica et Georgica* is dated "Charterhouse, Godalming, December 1897."

Gist of the poem is that Becker—"noble, open-faced, with wonderful eyes"—plays a concert with such bravura that the boys cover their ears; their reaction causes Robinson—"an attractive and most delightful man"—to smile; and thus does Charterhouse lack harmony.

Concerning his schooldays, Max said: "Charterhouse in the eighteen-eighties did not at all tend [to repress individuality in a child]. . . . Its traditions left plenty of latitude. I was a queer child. I didn't care a brass farthing for games. What I liked was Latin prose, Latin verse, and drawing caricatures."—Cf. "Old Carthusian Memories," *Mainly on the Air* (London, 1946), p. 92.

In Max's 7, 8 the first edition prints *"nota"* and "notum" with a breve over each "o." In his last note it has *"Carthusiana Domus."*

§ 2. *Elegiac couplets on Charterhouse*

"Old Carthusian Memories," *Mainly on the Air* (London, 1946), p. 89. Composed 1890, in Max's first term at Oxford. Title supplied by editor. The essay was written in 1920, and first published in *The Carthusian* (December 1920), pp. 34-35.

Of his lament Max said: ". . . the verses were an unpardonable libel on my views. I thought Charterhouse a very fine school really. . . . But—no, I was *not* [an Old Carthusian] of the straitest sect. My delight in having been at Charterhouse was far greater than had been my delight in being there."—*(op. cit.,* p. 89.)

Gist of the verses is that Charterhouse, once the worst of London's disasters, has flourished through countless years; flourishes now on its airy hilltop, teaching five hundred boys sadness; and will flourish as a reminder that hell awaits.

§ 3. *On W. S. Gilbert*

Autograph lines written on p. 17 of a copy of William S. Gilbert's *Songs of a Savoyard* (London, 1890) in the Beerbohm Collection in the Library of Merton College, Oxford (Provisional Catalogue No. 3.34). Title supplied by editor.

Gist of Beerbohm's comment, following the quoted wonderful-to-tell tag, is that Gilbert himself has realized his faults. The lines are accompanied by a drawing of a hand pointing to the last stanza of a song by Gilbert printed on the same page, as follows:

> I'm sure I'm no ascetic: I'm as pleasant as can be;
> You'll always find me ready with a crushing repartee;
> I've an irritating chuckle, I've a celebrated sneer,
> I've an entertaining snigger, I've a fascinating leer;
> To everybody's prejudice I know a thing or two;

I can tell a woman's age in half a minute—and I do—
But although I try to make myself as pleasant as I can,
Yet everybody says I'm such a disagreeable man!
    And I can't think why!

§ 4. *Damnosa Senectus*

Autograph lines, signed "H. M. B.," written in Beerbohm's early hand
on pp. 18-19 of the copy of William S. Gilbert's *Songs of a Savoyard*
referred to in the previous note. In the manuscript the original text of
line 6 of stanza 2 has been canceled and replaced by the present text,
which is in Beerbohm's later hand. Other, minor, revisions are in his
early hand.

The verses are a translation of Gilbert's "The Coming Bye and Bye,"
printed on pp. 18-19 of *Songs of a Savoyard*, as follows:

Sad is that woman's lot who, year by year,
Sees, one by one, her beauties disappear;
As Time, grown weary of her heart-drawn sighs,
Impatiently begins to "dim her eyes"!—
Herself compelled, in life's uncertain gloamings,
To wreathe her wrinkled brow with well saved "combings,"—
Reduced, with rouge, lipsalve, and pearly grey,
To "make up" for lost time, as best she may!

Silvered is the raven hair,
    Spreading is the parting straight,
Mottled the complexion fair,
    Halting is the youthful gait.
Hollow is the laughter free,
    Spectacled the limpid eye,
Little will be left of me,
    In the coming bye and bye!

Fading is the taper waist—
    Shapeless grows the shapely limb,
And although securely laced,
    Spreading is the figure trim!
Stouter than I used to be,
    Still more corpulent grow I—
There will be too much of me
    In the coming bye and bye!

§ 5. *Rondeau d'Admonition*

Text from the autograph manuscript owned by Mr. Simon Nowell-Smith, Oxford. The writing is in Beerbohm's early hand, and the poem is illustrated with a drawing. Added at bottom in a different hand are the words: "By Max at Oxford 1890-3." Turner was Max's closest friend, and they carried on a steady correspondence "from 1892, when they met at Merton, until Turner's death in 1938."—S. N. Behrman, *Conversation with Max* (London, 1960), p. 183; *idem, Portrait of Max* (New York, 1960), p. 218.

Line 10: "rollers," *i.e.,* roll call. Mr. Nowell-Smith writes: "In my day at Oxford (as in the day of Mr. Verdant Green) we slipped a pair of trousers and a mackintosh (buttoned to the neck) over our pyjamas and attended 'rollers' before going back to bed: nowadays, my sons tell me, neither rollers nor chapel is compulsory."

§ 6. *Ballade de la Vie Joyeuse*

Written on the verso of the title page of Reginald Turner's copy of Oscar Wilde's *The Picture of Dorian Gray* (London, 1891), now in the Harvard College Library (EC9.B3927.Z891w). The manuscript is in Beerbohm's early hand.

Stanza 2, line 5: the ms. omits the comma after "my friends."

§ 7. *'Doubt Divine'*

Written in Reginald Turner's copy of *The Book of the Rhymers' Club* (London, 1892), now in the Harvard College Library (EC9.B3927.Z892r). The poem, which is signed "P. O. E. Taster," is written in Beerbohm's early hand and is illustrated with a drawing.

In line 6 the ms. reads "e'er."

§ 8. *In Max's copy of J. K. Stephen's* Lapsus Calami

Reproduced in Sotheby's *Catalogue of the Library and Literary Manuscripts of the late Sir Max Beerbohm* (1960), p. 59. Title supplied by editor.

Lapsus Calami was published in 1891.

Line 1: Charles Stuart Calverley (1831-1884) and James Kenneth Stephen (1859-1892), British writers of parodies and humorous verse, known as "C. S. C." and "J. K. S." There are no periods after the initials in the ms.

§ 9. *On the imprint of the first English edition of* The Works of Max Beerbohm

Title supplied by editor. The last two lines have been written under the imprint of a presentation copy of the first English edition of *The Works of Max Beerbohm* (London, New York, 1896), inscribed by the Author: "For Reg [Turner] from Max 96." This copy is now in the library of Sir Geoffrey Keynes, M.A., M.D., F.R.C.S., Brinkley, Newmarket, Suffolk.

The period after the imprint supplied by the editor.

§ 10. *On a performance of* Ali Baba and the Forty Thieves

The Saturday Review (London), 31 December 1898, p. 878 ("Two Pantomimes"). Title supplied by editor.

Line 4: Arthur Collins was a leading producer of pantomimes.

§ 11. *An appreciation of Professor Mueller*

The Glasgow *Evening Citizen* of 21 April 1950, p. 5, reporting the Tory Osbert Peake's comments on the budget, said it reminded him (Peake) of this limerick ascribed to Max Beerbohm. Title supplied by editor.

Line 2: Max Müller (1823-1900), orientalist and philologist, first professor of comparative philology at Oxford.

§ 12. *In Max's copy of William Rothenstein's* Goya

Autograph manuscript on p. 39 of Beerbohm's copy of William Rothenstein's *Goya* (Artist's Library Series IV, London, 1900), now in the Beerbohm Collection, Library of Merton College, Oxford (Provisional Catalogue No. 3.71). Title supplied by editor.

§ 13. *Ballade of 'Another Luminary'*

Communicated by Lord David Cecil, Oxford. Signed "Max—1901." The autograph manuscript sold at the Sotheby sale (Sotheby's *Catalogue*, p. 80) is dated 1906.

The ballade is a satire on a number of popular writers of the period. Jerome Klapka Jerome (1859-1927), author of *Three Men in a Boat*, etc., and the play *The Passing of the Third Floor Back*; Barry Eric Odell Pain (1864-1928), author of *Eliza* and other humorous sketches of low life, and Jerome's successor as editor of *To-Day* (1897-1899); Albert Dresden Vandam (1843-1903), journalist, author of *An Englishman in Paris*, etc.; Robert Barr

(1850-1912), novelist and collaborator with Jerome in founding *The Idler* (1892-1911). "Nathaniel Gubbins" was first used as the pen-name of Edward Spencer, columnist on *The Sporting Times* (known as the *Pink 'Un*, because of the color of its newsprint). Mr. Greening was the head of Greening & Co., publishing firm of the day which specialized in pot-boilers and "shilling shockers." I have been unable to identify "Jimmy Davis"—unless he was Lieutenant-Colonel N. Newnham Davis who wrote for both *The Sporting Times* (the *Pink 'Un*) and *The Pall Mall Gazette*.

Nor do I know who "Mr. Turner" was, but ranking him second only to J. K. Jerome was an inverse compliment: seven years later Max was to inveigh against Jerome for being a prolific "tenth-rater" who "plasters [his humour] about with a liberal hand."—*Cf.* "A Deplorable Affair," *Around Theatres*, Vol. II (London, 1924), pp. 383-388.

Stanza 1, line 4: Lord David Cecil's typescript has a breve over the "o" of the first "Jerome," and a macron over the "o" of the second "Jerome."

Stanza 2, line 3: "par": journalistic colloquialism for a paragraph of rather unimportant prose.

§ 14. *To Dick*

Postcard from Beerbohm to Richard Le Gallienne, dated "Max 1902." Facsimile reproduction in Richard Le Gallienne, *The Romantic '90s* (London, 1926), p. 171.

§ 15. *Autobiography*

Written by Max in his copy of *Biography for Beginners* (1905) by Edmund Clerihew Bentley and G. K. Chesterton. Title supplied by editor. Printed in Sotheby's *Catalogue*, p. 17.

Bentley (1875-1956), more lastingly known for his classic detective novel *Trent's Last Case*, originated a type of humorous pseudo-biographical verse, usually in four lines of varying length, which became known as a "clerihew." Max uses this form here.

§ 16. *After Kipling's* Barrack-Room Ballads

"P.C., X, 36, by R*d**rd K*pl*ng," *A Christmas Garland* (London, 1912), p. 13. Title supplied by editor. The parody "P.C., X, 36" was first published in *The Saturday Review* (London), 15 December 1906, pp. 736-737. Beerbohm owned a copy of Kipling's *Barrack-Room Ballads* (1892); *(see* Sotheby's *Catalogue,* p. 39).

§ 17. *Triolets by A. C. B.*

Lines in parody of A. C. Benson, written in Max's copy of Benson's *Beside Still Waters* (1907), and signed "Max Beerbohm." This copy is now in the University of California Library, Los Angeles. The Sotheby *Catalogue* records an autograph manuscript (1 p., 4*to*) of these triolets, with the subtitle: "To be inscribed in any volume of his Essays" (p. 78).

Arthur Christopher Benson (1862-1925), a voluminous writer and master of Magdalene College, Cambridge. He was the son of Edward White Benson (1829-1896), archbishop of Canterbury.

§ 18. *Chorus of a song that might have been written by Albert Chevalier*

"Music Halls of My Youth," *Mainly on the Air* (London, 1946), p. 43. Title supplied by editor. "Music Halls of My Youth" was broadcast 18 January 1942 and the chorus was sung by Max.

Albert Chevalier (1861-1923) was a famous British music-hall comedian. Max writes: "I had the pleasure of meeting him once, in his later years, and was sorely tempted to offer him an idea which might well have been conceived by himself: a song about a publican whom the singer had known and revered, who was now dead, whose business was carried on by his son, Ben, an excellent young man,—'But 'e'll never be the man 'is Father woz.' The chorus was to be something of this sort: [follows text of chorus]."—*Ibid.,* pp. 42-43.

§ 19. *To Henry James*

From the photocopy of the autograph manuscript in the Beerbohm Collection, Library of Merton College, Oxford (Provisional Catalogue No. 7.8). Reproduced in Evan Charteris, *The Life and Letters of Sir Edmund Gosse* (London, 1931), plate facing p. 398.

Line 1: the ms. spells "indefatiguable."

"Max Beerbohm had started a game which he played with Gosse, by the terms of which a sonnet was sent to and fro by post till each writer had contributed his quota of alternate lines."—*(op. cit.,* p. 390).

From a letter written by Gosse to Beerbohm, dated Bowness-on-Windermere, 30 June 1916: "As to our sonnet, I can no longer recapture my own share in it. Our two mighty brains melted into one over it, like the vast clouds on the brow of Helvellyn. (I like to be local.) . . . this great sonnet; in which the twin strands of our geniuses are so inextricably woven. . . . In this sonnet we stand forth to Posterity as the Great Siamese Twins of Sentiment, 'with careless ostentation shouldering' one another, as Wordsworth so beautifully said. . . ."—(*loc. cit.*)

From a note on this sonnet written by Beerbohm to Evan Charteris: "I am not sure whether it was Walter Raleigh or I that invented the Sonnet game. I often played it—sometimes in a room, sometimes by post. In the Spring of 1908 Gosse offered to play a round with me. We played it by post—by return of post, every time. I wrote the first line, Gosse the second. The even-numbered lines are his, and the odd-numbered mine." —(*op. cit.*, plate facing p. 398.)

The following passage from a letter written by Beerbohm to Gosse from 48, Upper Berkeley Street, W., dated "Monday night," also refers to this sonnet game: "Before going to bed, I send you the current line of our sonnet; with very many thanks for the lovely evening I have had. On Wednesday morning I go to Dieppe. At our present rate of progress, you will receive the penultimate line just then. Please convey the ultimate to me at the Hôtel du Rhin. Your proud collaborator Max." (Letter in the Brotherton Collection, The Brotherton Library, University of Leeds.)

Nos. 22 and 49, 50, 51, 52, 53 and 54 are other examples of the game; but played with other friends.

§ 20. *In his own copy of* Caricatures of Twenty-Five Gentlemen

After his name on the half-title Max has written: "and by him coloured in the year of grace 1909," followed by the two lines of verse. *Caricatures of Twenty-Five Gentlemen* was published in 1896.

Title supplied by editor. Reproduced in Sotheby's *Catalogue*, p. 6.

§ 21. *Specimen Chapter of Forthcoming Work* Half Hours with the Dialects of England

Printed from the typescript, with revisions and additions in Beerbohm's hand, in the Harvard College Library.

Although the typescript and autograph insertions employ initial double quotation marks throughout—as was Beerbohm's usual personal style for such punctuation—the single quotation mark has been substituted by the editor to make "A Specimen Chapter" conform in style to that of selections from printed sources. This change has been made elsewhere.

The reference in line 13 of the sonnet is to Henry James's tragic master-piece *The Wings of the Dove* (1902), which was written at Rye, where he had leased a house in 1897 in order to work uninterrupted by the social distractions he enjoyed in London.

For another of Max's excursions into dialect, *see* No. 28.

§ 22. *Lines to be Hung in a Hotel Bedroom at Charing Cross*

Marguerite Steen, *William Nicholson* (London, 1943), pp. 90-91.

"Their chief form of diversion was writing sonnets, of the kind that the euphemism of booksellers' advertisements classifies as 'curious.' At this game William [Nicholson], Max and Pamela von Hutten excelled; Max, in fact, was pulverised by the sudden discovery of his own talent in this direction. 'Really—I have to tear them up and watch them well on their way to the sea before I can regard myself as fit to mix with decent society!' he is reported to have said. The method of production of these works of literature was each player alternately to contribute a line; unfortunately, they are quite unreproducible. Their quality may be judged from a few surviving stanzas of the *Lines to be Hung in a Hotel Bedroom at Charing Cross*. It was the year of Blériot's flight across the Channel, when Monsieur and Madame Blériot were reported to have spent the night at the Charing Cross Hotel. The first line runs: [text of first part quoted]—after which William's memory discreetly fails him, but for the concluding fragment: [follows text of the last two parts]."—*Ibid.*, p. 90.

Nos. 19 and 49 through 54 are also products of Max's sonnet game.

§ 23. *Invocation to Luther*

Autograph draft, with variant discarded readings, in Beerbohm's review copy of G. K. Chesterton's *George Bernard Shaw* (1909), which he has inscribed to his friend Reginald Turner: "For Reg | Affectionately | Max | 1909." Property of Mr. Jay Hall, Statesville, North Carolina. Title supplied by editor.

This sonnet apparently never got resolved. It is written in pencil, and the following words are difficult to make out: "base" (line 6), "grins" (line 9), "d'Hartepoint" and "Brontë" (line 10). There are arabic numerals at some of the lines to the right of the script; and at the left, a list of possible rhymes: "wall, small, call, thrall, crawl, fall." After line 6 I have omitted the words "the land"; after line 9 I have omitted the line "And

. . . laughs into his brindled beard."

Line 9: Henry Fitzalan-Howard, fifteenth Duke of Norfolk, Earl of Arundel (1847-1917), was the leader of the English Roman Catholics.

I have been unable to identify the Marquis d'Hartepoint. The name may be fictitious.

§ 24. *In Max's top hat*

Title supplied by editor.

In his tribute to Sir Max Beerbohm on his eightieth birthday (*The Listener*, 28 August 1952, p. 338) Robert Graves writes: "At the close of the 1914-18 war I became son-in-law to William Nicholson—Kid Nicholson—who kept a collection of discarded hats in his studio at Appletree Yard, St. James's. At his request I hung up my steel helmet as an *ex voto* offering on the peg next to a certain superbly glossy top-hat. I had the curiosity to look at the lining. Inside was your visiting card. It commemorated your abandonment of London club life when you went to live in Italy. You had written: . . . [follows text of poem]."

Reprinted in S. N. Behrman, *Conversation with Max* (London, 1960), p. 195; *idem, Portrait of Max* (New York, 1960), p. 233.

§ 25. *In a letter to Edmund Gosse*

Title supplied by editor. The verses occur in a letter written by Beerbohm to Edmund Gosse, dated "12 Well Walk, Hampstead N. W., Jan. 26, 1917" [= 1918, for the envelope is stamped 26 Jan. 18], and preserved in the British Museum, London (Ashley MS A. 100). The poem must have been written some time before the First World War, because Max, after quoting the verses, continues: "But alas, how long ago it seems, the time when I had that pleasure, commingled with that pity! Down, down came Lady S. with awful suddenness, owing to the mad folly of the German Emperor; and purged away by her fall is all that there was of bitter in the hearts of the two Lady Ms."

Line 1: wife of Sir Edgar Speyer (1862-1932), financier, philanthropist, and patron of music. The son of a German-Jewish banker, Sir Edgar's patriotism was called into question at the outbreak of the First World War.

Line 4: wife of Alfred Moritz Mond, first Baron Melchett (1868-1930), industrialist, financier, and politician.

Line 5: wife of (?) Sir William Stevenson Meyer (1860-1922), the first High Commissioner of India.

§ 26. *The Characters of Shakespeare*

The Mask (Florence), July 1924, p. 119. The autograph manuscript owned by Mr. Joseph M. Bransten, San Francisco, California (1 p., folio, written in pencil, with revisions), has a different text. The stanza beginning "The other Shakespearean characters . . ." has been added from it.

Stanza 1, lines 1-2: the references are to Charles Lamb (1775-1834), author of "On the Tragedies of Shakespeare" (1811); Samuel Taylor Coleridge (1772-1834), poet and critic; August Wilhelm von Schlegel (1767-1845), German poet, Shakespeare translator and critic, author of *Vorlesungen über dramatische Kunst und Literatur* (1809-11); Edward Dowden (1843-1913), author of *Shakespere: A Critical Study of his Mind and Art* (1875); and Sir Sidney Lee (1859-1926), author of *A Life of William Shakespeare* (1898).

Last stanza, line 2: E. G. C.: Edward Gordon Craig (b. 1872), British theatrical producer, stage designer, and writer on the art of the theater. He lived at the Villa Reggio, Rapallo, adjacent to Beerbohm's house.

§ 27. *Epistle by the Duke to his heir presumptive*

Zuleika Dobson (London, 1911), p. 201. Title supplied by editor. Gist of the fragment: "wretched is the man unwary of feminine wiles, for there is no safety but that a woman can betray it, no faith but that . . ."

§ 28. *To an Undergraduate Needing Rooms in Oxford*

Zuleika Dobson (London, 1911), p. 264. Composed by the Duke as a testimonial for his landlady Mrs. Batch. Beerbohm continues: "I do not quote the poem *in extenso*, because, frankly, I think it was one of his least happily inspired works."

§ 29. *After Hilaire Belloc*

"Of Christmas, by H*l**re B*ll*c," *A Christmas Garland* (London, 1912), pp. 150-151. Title to this parody supplied by the editor.

§ 30. *Again—after Hilaire Belloc*

"Of Christmas, by H*l**re B*ll*c," *A Christmas Garland* (London, 1912), p. 151. Title to this parody supplied by the editor.

§ 31. *A Sequelula to* The Dynasts

A Christmas Garland (Collected edition, vol. V, London, 1922), pp. 53-66. First edition 1912. The Douglas Cleverdon adaptation was broadcast in June 1951.

Page 39: Clement King Shorter (1857-1926), journalist and critic, author of two books on Napoleon: *Napoleon and his Fellow-Travellers* (1908) and *Napoleon in his own Defence* (1910).

§ 32. *Ballade of an Illustrious Freshman*

Communicated by Lord David Cecil. The autograph manuscript is signed *"M."*

The occasion of this ballade was the Prince of Wales's visit to Oxford University on 12-13 October 1912 to become a freshman there and to join in the everyday life of the University as an ordinary student.

Line 3: Edward, Prince of Wales: the present Duke of Windsor.

Line 4: Henry Peter Hansell (1863-1935) was the Prince's tutor and already resident at Magdalen College, Oxford.

§ 33. *Elegy on Any Lady*

From the autograph manuscript in the Harvard College Library (fMS Eng 696.14).

Beerbohm wrote the same verses in his presentation copy of the third volume, *Salve* (1912), of George Moore's *"Hail and Farewell!"* (1911-1914). They are reproduced on p. 45 of Sotheby's *Catalogue,* under a slightly different title ("Elegy on *any* Lady | by | G. M."), and with three dots instead of a full stop after line 3. Also printed in Bohun Lynch, *Max Beerbohm in Perspective* (London, 1921), p. 23, under the title "Elegy on *Any* Lady."

It is known that George Moore was always chattering about imaginary love affairs.

§ 34. *Ballade Tragique à Double Refrain*

From the autograph manuscript, Ashley MS 5155, in the British Museum, London. In line 3 the ms. reads "Allen."

The Monarchs referred to are George V and Queen Mary.

Stanza 5, line 6: Josephine de Beauharnais, wife of Napoleon I.

According to T. J. Wise the poem was written in 1912. Beerbohm gave ms. copies of it to several friends, and a few copies were printed by Harold Monro, for private circulation, on one side of a single leaf of thin paper, no place, no date, no printer's or publisher's imprint. The text of the broadside is slightly different from the text of the ms. The edition was never authorized by Beerbohm. Reproduced in facsimile in *The Ashley Library: A Catalogue of Printed Books, Manuscripts and Autograph Letters Collected by Thomas James Wise* (London, privately printed), vol. X (1930), facing p. 14. Printed, with minor variants, in S. N. Behrman, *Conversation with Max* (London, 1960), pp. 82-83; *idem, Portrait of Max* (New York, 1960), pp. 100-101.

§ 35. *To a Young Woman*

Published in "Enoch Soames," *Seven Men* (London, 1919), p. 16. The autograph manuscript of "Enoch Soames," which was written in 1912, is in Yale University Library.

See also Nos. 36 and 70.

§ 36. *Nocturne*

Published in "Enoch Soames," *Seven Men* (London, 1919), p. 17.

See also Nos. 35 and 70.

§ 37. *Drinking Song*

Published, with the exception of the second stanza, in "Playgoing," *Mainly on the Air* (London, 1946), pp. 68-69. The second stanza has been taken from the slightly different version of "Drinking Song" that occurs in Doris Arthur Jones, *The Life and Letters of Henry Arthur Jones* (London, 1930), pp. 253-254. "Playgoing" was broadcast 8 October 1945, but the verses were written about 1912.

Stanza 1, line 9: Jack Thomas Grein (1862-1935), who founded the Independent Theatre and performed Ibsen's *Ghosts* in 1891.

Stanza 2, line 1: Hermann Sudermann (1857-1928), German dramatist and novelist.

_____ line 3: José Echegaray y Eizaguirre (1832-1916), Spanish dramatist.

_____ line 4: *i.e.*, Björnstjerne Martinius Björnson (1832-1910), Norwegian dramatist.

Stanza 3, lines 3-5: Sir Arthur Wing Pinero (1855-1934) and Henry Arthur Jones (1851-1929), British dramatists; William Archer (1856-1924), British dramatic critic and playwright.

§ 38. *A Ballade of Judges*

Autograph manuscript, signed "*Mx*," owned by Professor Majel Ewing, Los Angeles, California.

§ 39. *In a copy of More's (or Shaw's or Wells's or Plato's or anybody's) Utopia*

Written on the verso of the autograph manuscript of "A Ballade of Judges," for which see preceding note. Printed in Sotheby's *Catalogue*, p. 79.

§ 40. *Mr. John Masefield*

Fifty Caricatures (London, 1913), plate 12, dated 1913.

§ 41. *A Ballade of My Betters*

From the autograph rough draft, with revisions and deletions, in the Harvard College Library (MS Eng 696.16). The title, the first stanza, and the word "Envoi" have been supplied from the copy owned by Lord David Cecil, Oxford.

Stanza 2, line 2: I suggest "stylo," but the word is difficult to read.
—— line 4: Reginald John Campbell (1867-1956), author of *The New Theology* (1907).

Stanza 3, line 2: Sir Edward Grey, Viscount of Fallodon (1862-1933), Foreign Secretary 1905-1916.

§ 42. *On the Uniform Edition of the works of George Meredith*

The Works of Max Beerbohm (Collected edition, vol. I, London, 1922), p. ix (Preface). Title supplied by editor.

In this preface to the first volume of *his* uniform edition, Max deplored the "very handsome . . . very monumental and memorial and definitive" tomes of the specially published "sets" that tended to entomb old favorites and deny them the vitality they possessed in earlier—and more modest—editions.—(*loc. cit.*)

Nos. 43 and 44 are in the same vein.

§ 43. *On the Uniform Edition of the works of Henry James*

The Works of Max Beerbohm (Collected edition, vol. I., London, 1922), p. x (Preface). Title supplied by editor.

§ 44. *On the Uniform Edition of the works of R. L. Stevenson*

The Works of Max Beerbohm (Collected edition, vol. I, London, 1922), p. x (Preface). Title supplied by editor. I have changed "*Çi git*" to "*Ci-git.*"

§ 45. *A Ballade* ad hoc

Typescript owned by Lord David Cecil, Oxford.

Stanza 2, line 7: Johann Peter Eckermann (1792-1854), German poet and author.

Stanza 3, line 1: Brian Boru (926-1014), King of Ireland, also known as Brian Boruma, or Boroimhe.

§ 46. *To W. S.——1914*

Autograph manuscript owned by Mr. William A. von Metz, Oakland, California. The copy owned by Lord David Cecil, Oxford, is inscribed: "My dear Walter | Line 8 of this sonnet is | yours—do you remember? | The rest isn't worthy of it, but | is mine. Yours ever Max. | In lines 10 and 13 the rhyme is | of course a double one—the stress comes on *few* and *new*." Mr. von Metz's typescript version of this sonnet, headed "To Walter Sickert 1913," and an autograph manuscript version in the Harvard College Library (fMS Eng 696.14), headed "To Walter Sickert" and dated June 1914, show minor textual variants.

Line 1: Walter Richard Sickert (1860-1942), British painter.

Line 5: George Francis Miles (1852-1891), British painter; James Abbott McNeill Whistler (1834-1903), American painter and etcher.

Line 6: Percy William Justyne (1812-1883), British artist and book illustrator (?); Sir Henry Irving (1838-1905), British actor-manager.

Line 7: George Leybourne (1842-1884), British music-hall performer. His real name was Joe Saunders.

Line 14: *Blast: Review of the Great English Vortex*, an avant-garde periodical edited by Wyndham Lewis. Only two numbers were published, No. 1 on 20 June 1914, No. 2 in July 1915.

§ 47. *Brave Rover*

From the autograph manuscript on Iles Farm letterhead in the Harvard College Library (fMS Eng 696.14).

Written at Iles Farm, Far Oakridge, Stroud, Gloucestershire, where the Beerbohms lived with William and Alice Rothenstein during the First

World War. The Rothensteins' dog was called Rover. The references are to Rachel, eldest daughter of William Rothenstein; Betty, his second daughter; William Michael, his second son; John, his elder son, later the Director of the Tate Gallery; Charles Lambert, William Rothenstein's elder brother, who lived in Bradford, Yorkshire; and Albert, his younger brother, who lived at Lincoln's Inn, London, from about 1917 to 1918, or possibly later.

Printed, with a slightly different punctuation, in William Rothenstein, *Men and Memories, 1900-1922* (London, 1932), pp. 313-314.

Though the Beerbohms had moved to Italy, they preferred to return when England was in distress; they also returned in 1938, until 1947.

§ 48. *Thomas Hardy and A. E. Housman*

William Rothenstein, *Men and Memories, 1900-1922* (London, 1932), p. 343. The 1934 edition of this book has a slightly different text.

Beerbohm wrote these lines in a book Housman gave to William Rothenstein. Housman came sometimes to stay at Woodchester, when he would walk over to Oakridge; and Rothenstein was more than once his guest at Cambridge.

§ 49. *To Rabindranath Tagore*

Robert Speaight, *William Rothenstein: The Portrait of an Artist in his Time* (London, 1962), pp. 259-260. Title supplied by the editor.

In the summer of 1912 Rothenstein did six portrait drawings of Tagore. This irreverent sonnet was composed at Far Oakridge (where the Beerbohms lived with, and then near by, the Rothensteins during the First War), a few years after Tagore had left England. Lines 1, 4, 7, 10, 13 were written by Mrs. Alice Rothenstein; and lines 3, 6, 9, 12 by William Rothenstein. I have added a comma after line 5.

Line 14: Sir William Newenham Montague Orpen (1878-1931), British painter.

Other productions of Max's game during this period are a series presented as Nos. 50, 51, 52, 53 and 54. Earlier sonnets, "played" with Edmund Gosse and William Nicholson, are Nos. 19 and 22, respectively.

§ 50. *Iles Farm, Far Oakridge*

This sonnet forms, with the following four (Nos. 51, 52, 53 and 54), a series of five *bouts-rimés*, exercises or games participated in by Beerbohm and William Rothenstein during the First World War, when they lived at Far Oakridge, Stroud, Gloucestershire. The rough drafts of these poems are preserved in the Harvard College Library (fMS Eng 696.14). The title has been supplied by the editor.

In these rough drafts the punctuation is naturally somewhat scrappy, therefore I have taken the liberty of inserting a period or a comma here and there.

Line 6: the "City of the Violet Crown": Athens, so called by Pindar and Aristophanes.

Line 10: Iles Farm, an old farmhouse at Far Oakridge, which the Rothensteins had bought and where they lived from 1912 to 1920.

§ 51. *To the Rev. Percy Dearmer*

Autograph draft in the Harvard College Library (fMS Eng 696.14). *(See also* Nos. 50, 52, 53 and 54: the other "game" sonnets in this series played with William Rothenstein.)

The title, as well as the odd lines, are in Beerbohm's hand.

Percy Dearmer (1867-1936), British divine. His first wife died in 1915, and he married again in 1916.

§ 52. *Frau Krupp's 'little dears'*

Autograph draft in the Harvard College Library (fMS Eng 696.14). Title supplied by the editor.

Line 5: the ms. spells "Terries" and "Marian." The references are to Dame Ellen Terry (1847-1928), to her sisters Marion (1852-1930), Kate (1844-1924), and Florence (1854-1896), and to her brother Fred (1863-1933), all of whom went on the stage. Ellen Terry lived at Smallhythe, Tenterden, Kent, during 1915-1918.

Line 10: the ms. has the archaic spelling "Escalibar."

Line 13: Bertha Krupp von Bohlen und Halbach (1886-1957), head of the German firm of Krupp, manufacturers of armor and guns. She is represented as referring to the bombs as "my little dears."

This poem is the third in a series of *bouts-rimés (see* Nos. 50, 51, 53, 54) and one of eight such sonnets in this book *(see also* 19, 22 and 49).

§ 53. *Eli the Thatcher*

Autograph draft in the Harvard College Library (fMS Eng 696.14). Title supplied by editor. The sonnet is apparently unfinished.

Line 2: Eli, the name of an old thatcher at Far Oakridge. William Rothenstein's pencil drawing of Eli, made in 1913, is reproduced in Robert Speaight, *William Rothenstein: The Portrait of an Artist in his Time* (London, 1962), plate facing p. 304. The drawing is now in the City Art Galleries, Manchester.

Other Beerbohm-Rothenstein compositions are Nos. 49-52 and 54 (*see also* 19 and 22).

§ 54. *To Max on his taking his only walk at Oakridge*

Autograph draft, Harvard College Library (fMS Eng 696.14).

Lines 3, 6, 9 and 12 are in Beerbohm's hand; lines 1, 4, 7, 10, 13 in Rothenstein's hand; lines 2, 5, 8, 11, 14 are in an unidentified hand. Line 14 has been compounded from a number of variants in the manuscript. Title added by Rothenstein.

Line 2: Rover was the name of the Rothensteins' dog.

Line 3: Kate Rorke (1866-1945), a well-known British actress. She played a very large number of parts in her long career, including Ophelia in *Hamlet* and Lady Percy in *Henry IV, Part I*, but I have been unable to find a record of her playing the part of Rosalind.

Line 12: "our dear King": George V. There was of course no basis in fact for the melodrama implied in this allusion to a Sovereign acclaimed for his rectitude. As in No. 52, Max's impish *non sequiturs* were designed to challenge the author of the succeeding line.

This poem is the last sonnet-game composition (*see* Nos. 19, 22, 49-53).

§ 55. *On the origin of the name* Cirencester

From the autograph manuscript in the Harvard College Library (fMS Eng 696.14). The title has been supplied by the editor. Lord David Cecil, Oxford, owns a copy with a slightly different text.

The title of the manuscript, "Poems on the Nomenclature of the Various Towns and Villages around Oakridge. I.," suggests that Max planned a series of similar pieces.

Probably written during the First World War, when Max and Florence Beerbohm lived with the Rothensteins at Far Oakridge, Stroud, Gloucestershire.

Stanza 4, lines 1-2 refer to Iles Farm, Far Oakridge, the Rothensteins' home from 1912 to 1920.

Last stanza, last line: the ms. spells SYREN'S SISTER.

§ 56. *Lines on a certain Friend's remarkable Faculty for swift Generalisation*

Autograph verses on William Rothenstein, written on half-title verso of Beerbohm's copy of Rothenstein's *Goya* (Artist's Library Series IV, London, 1900), now in the Beerbohm Collection, Library of Merton College, Oxford (Provisional Catalogue No. 3.71). The poem is signed and dated "M B | Far Oakridge | 1916." Max and Florence Beerbohm lived with the Rothensteins at Far Oakridge, Stroud, Gloucestershire, during the First World War.

Published, with one or two textual variants, in William Rothenstein, *Since Fifty: Men and Memories, 1922-1938* (London, 1939), p. 258; in S. N. Behrman, *Conversation with Max* (London, 1960), p. 71; *idem, Portrait of Max* (New York, 1960), pp. 87-88; and in Robert Speaight, *William Rothenstein: The Portrait of an Artist in his Time* (London, 1962), p. 334.

"These lines were written when we played parlour games with pen and pencil. Max and Ellis Roberts are masters at improvisation. Ellis would read out our composite verses with sonorous voice and rolling eye, adding thereby to the uproarious hilarity."—(Rothenstein, *loc. cit.*).

According to Max, Rothenstein was very resilient in mood—"always matching your own, don't you know."—(Behrman, *op. cit.*, p. 70; *idem, op. cit.*, p. 87.)

§ 57. *Same Cottage—but Another Song, of Another Season*

Published in William Rothenstein, *Men and Memories, 1900-1922* (London, 1932), pp. 324-325; reprinted, under the title "Back to Town," in *Literary Digest* (New York), 6 August 1932, p. 38.

On the authority of a reproduction of an autograph manuscript of the first stanza of this poem in Sotheby's *Catalogue* (p. 21) I have changed the word "her" in line 4 to "its."

The verses parody a poem by John Drinkwater, whose lyric memory of his summer (1917) spent in the Rothensteins' cottage at Far Oakridge follows:

Cottage Song

Morning and night I bring
Clear water from the spring,
And through the lyric noon
I hear the larks in tune,

And when the shadows fall
There's providence for all.

My garden is alight
With currants red and white,
And my blue curtains peep
On starry courses deep,
While down her silver tides
The moon on Cotswold rides.

My path of paven grey
Is thoroughfare all day
For fellowship, till time
Bids us with candles climb
The little whitewashed stair
Above my lavender.
                        Tides (London, 1917), p. 38.

Max, who remembered his own tribulations during a wartime winter in the same cottage (*see* Note 49), promptly composed his rebuttal and inscribed it: "For J. D. from M. B. August 4. 1917 with 1,000,000 apologies for this wicked echo of so lovely a poem."

§ 58. *After W. B. Yeats*

"First Meetings with W. B. Yeats," *Mainly on the Air*, new enlarged edition (London, 1957), pp. 95-96. Written about 1916; broadcast 26 December 1954. Title supplied by editor.

Max writes: "At Charterhouse, one morning, a small boy construed thus a rather difficult line of Euripides: 'And a tear shall lead the blind man.' 'H'm,' said his form-master, 'clever tear!' Thereat we all laughed. But ought we to have laughed? Granted, the translation was hopelessly inaccurate. But in itself was not the image beautiful, and expressed in terms simple and sensuous, if not passionate? I am led to ask this because, in after years, when first I read some of the poems of W. B. Yeats, those words came back to my memory, and seemed to have been inspired by his own Muse. 'And a tear shall lead the blind man' . . . how easily, how well (thought I, and still think), might some poem of this distinguished and true poet end just like that! [follows text of verse]."—*Ibid.*, p. 95.

§ 59. Savonarola: *A Tragedy by L. Brown*

From " 'Savonarola' Brown," *Seven Men* (Collected edition, vol. VII, London 1922), pp. 185-215, 217-218. First edition 1919. Written 1917. Autograph manuscript in Yale University Library.

Produced at the Haymarket Theatre, London, by Sir Nigel Playfair 25 February 1930 on behalf of the Oxford Preservation Fund. Adapted for broadcasting by John Cheatle in 1939, and by the Oxford University Dramatic Society in 1956.

Savonarola was a hit with the select audience who saw it in 1930. The following is from *The Times* (London) of 26 February 1930:

"Mr. Max Beerbohm's famous burlesque, that irresponsible, impossible, 'unactable' thing commonly called ' "Savonarola" Brown', now at last, by the ingenuity of Sir Nigel Playfair, who sat at a little table reading the stage directions, [is] brought to the theatre.

"How would it go? How would an audience denied a reader's opportunity to examine Mr. Beerbohm's wit and roll his bathos on a leisurely tongue receive this sport with the writers of pseudo-Elizabethan tragedy? A great part of the game is in the stage directions and in the actors' literal obedience to them, and this part Sir Nigel won in triumph aided and abetted by an occasional contretemps which he turned brilliantly to account.

"The other part of the game is in the extravagant lapses of the verse which, as no other verse in the world, has a habit of falling in a land-slide of absurdity from purple heights into the abyss."

§ 60. *Ballad of a recurring anomaly in Berkeley Square*

Communicated by Lord David Cecil, Oxford. The autograph manuscript recorded in Sotheby's *Catalogue* (p. 81) is inscribed: "Written in Harlech. Autumn 1918. Max Beerbohm."

The references in this poem are to Sir Squire Bancroft (1841-1926), British actor and theatrical manager, who rebuilt and opened the Haymarket Theatre in 1880; Valentine Baker (?) (1827-1887), British cavalry officer and writer on military subjects; Alfred Ernest Albert, Duke of Edinburgh (?) (1844-1900), second son of Queen Victoria and Prince Albert; Sir Edward Seymour George Hicks (1871-1949), British actor-manager and author, married to Ellaline Terriss; and Arthur Bourchier (1863-1927), British actor-manager. Arthur Bourchier was one of Max's chief objects of attack as a dramatic critic. His second wife, whom he married in 1918, was Violet Marion Kyrle Bellew.

Last stanza, last line: Harry Relph (1868-1928), British music-hall artist. He performed first as a black-face comedian, calling himself "Little Tichborne" after the claimant in the famous Tichborne Case. Later he dropped the black-face routine and abbreviated his name to "Little Tich." He was a short man, a fact he emphasized by wearing enormously large and long boots on his feet.

§ 61. *After Tom Moore*

Autograph manuscript, with revisions and deletions, dated 21 July 1920, owned by Mr. David Magee, San Francisco, California. Title supplied by editor.

"The white rose of theft and the red rose of arson" (line 1 of the opening stanza) is a phrase which occurs on p. 251 of Beerbohm's essay "The Crime," written in 1920 and published in *And Even Now* (London, 1920). At the head of the manuscript of this parody is a note by Max explaining that the phrase "sounds like a quotation from a poem by Tom Moore but I can't verify the poem, and so I have to write it, if possible."

§ 62. *In Max's copy of Housman's* A Shropshire Lad

Title supplied by editor. A. E. Housman's *A Shropshire Lad* appeared in 1896. The copy in which these autograph lines occur on half-title verso was published by Grant Richards, Ltd. in 1920. It is now in the Beerbohm Collection in the Library of Merton College, Oxford (Provisional Catalogue No. 3.57).

§ 63. *A Prayer*

Parody of the following poem by John Galsworthy titled "The Prayer":

> If on a Spring night I went by
> And God were standing there,
> What is the prayer I would cry
> To Him? This is the prayer:
>
> > 'O Lord of courage grave,
> > O Master of this night of Spring,
> > Make firm in me a heart too brave
> > To ask Thee anything!'
>
> *The Collected Poems of John Galsworthy* (London, 1934).

Both poems are printed, with a commentary, in Sir Edward Marsh, *A Number of People* (London, 1939), pp. 345-346. The text is taken from the facsimile reproduction in "Sir Edward Marsh's Little Book" in *The Saturday Book*, Eleventh Year, edited by Leonard Russell (London, 1951), pp. 176-177 ["Sir Edward Marsh's Little Book," pp. 159-182].

Sir Edward Howard Marsh (1872-1953) was private secretary to Winston Churchill and other Cabinet Ministers from 1905 to 1937.

"Lady Diana Cooper presented Sir Edward Marsh originally with the Little Book; and he prevailed upon some famous poets to fill its blank pages by copying out one of their own poems, usually their favourite. . . . One piece was written specially for the book—by Max Beerbohm, who wrote a parody of the poem by Galsworthy on the preceding page."—*The Saturday Book*, pp. 159-160.

Marsh's "little book" contains ninety-seven poems. Thomas Hardy, Rudyard Kipling, D. H. Lawrence, A. E. Housman, John Masefield, Rupert Brooke, Hilaire. Belloc and Walter de la Mare are among the poets who contributed to it. Max's poem is dated 27 April 1921.

§ 64. *Vague Lyric by G. M.*

Written by Beerbohm on the reverse of the contents page of his presentation copy from Sydney Pawling of George Moore's *Memoirs of my Dead Life* (revised and enlarged edition, 1921). Copy owned by Mr. Stephen Greene, West Dover, Vermont.

§ 65. *In a copy of W. J. Turner's* Paris and Helen

Autograph verses—written on half-title and signed "M. B."—in Florence Beerbohm's presentation copy of W. J. Turner's *Paris and Helen* (1921). Printed in Sotheby's *Catalogue*, p. 64. Title supplied by editor.

The copy cited is now in the Harvard College Library.

§ 66. *To H. G.-B.*

The first four stanzas are printed on a leaf pasted between the title page and p. v of Max's copy of Harley Granville-Barker's *The Exemplary Theatre* (London, 1922), now in the Beerbohm Collection, Merton College Library, Oxford (Provisional Catalogue No. 3.54); they are signed and dated "Max, | Rapallo, | March, 1922." The additional stanza is written by Beerbohm on the title page verso; it is signed and dated "Max 1923." In stanza 2, line 4 the printed leaf spells "Might-Have Beens." Another copy of *The Exemplary Theatre*, also in the Beerbohm Collection, contains a slightly different autograph version of the poem, however, without the additional stanza. The poem is published, with minor textual variants, in S. N. Behrman, *Conversation with Max* (London, 1960), pp. 160-161; *idem, Portrait of Max* (New York, 1960), pp. 191-192.

Harley Granville Granville-Barker (1877-1946) was a British actor, dramatist, and theatrical scholar.

In the Preface to *The Exemplary Theatre* Granville-Barker had written: ". . . it may well be that just as Shakespeare made of drama something which outspanned all its then acknowledged powers, so we, gathering up tradition with understanding and measuring our power by our need, might make in our turn of the theatre something that would not only better, but quite transcend, its present service to us."—(pp. xi-xii).

Stanza 3, line 7: L.C.C.: London County Council.

Stanza 4, line 4: William Poel (1852-1934), actor, stage director, and author. Poel revolutionized stage production by presenting without scenery seventeen of Shakespeare's plays. He wrote several plays himself, and also *Shakespeare and the Theatre* (1913).

§ 67. *Sir Herbert Vansittart*

"Studies in the Eighteen-Seventies," *Things New and Old* (London, 1923), plate 44. The caricature which contains these lines is supposed to have been drawn in 1873.

Sir Herbert Vansittart is an imaginary statesman. "Prinny": the public sobriquet for George Augustus Frederick (1762-1830) while Prince Regent for his father, George III, from 1811 until he became George IV in 1820.

§ 68. *Triolets composed on a day when I thought (from what he had said on a previous day) that Harley wouldn't turn up for luncheon*

From the autograph manuscript in the Harvard College Library (EC9. B3927.896we). The verses are signed and dated "Feb. 1923. Max" and refer to Harley Granville Granville-Barker, the actor, producer, dramatist, and Shakespeare critic. Granville-Barker's "Cymbeline" was published in his *Prefaces to Shakespeare: Second Series* (London, 1930).

Published in S. N. Behrman, *Conversation with Max* (London, 1960), pp. 156-157; *idem, Portrait of Max* (New York, 1960), pp. 187-188.

In 1918 Granville-Barker married Helen Huntington, a poet and novelist of some distinction.

§ 69. *A Luncheon*

Privately printed (25 numbered copies) for Mr. Simon Nowell-Smith by John Johnson, Oxford, September 1946. Text from Mr. Nowell-Smith's own copy No. 13.

A note on p. [4] of this pamphlet reads: "In the summer of 1923, when the Prince of Wales was about to pay his annual visit to the Duchy of Cornwall, someone at Court suggested to him that he should, on his way, visit Mr. Thomas Hardy. The Prince agreed to do so, and in due course lunched with Mr. and Mrs. Hardy. Hearing of this, Max Beerbohm composed the lines which, with his consent, are printed here." (The Prince of Wales referred to is the present Duke of Windsor.)

The Harvard College Library has a slightly different version of this poem, written in Beerbohm's autograph (fMS Eng 696.14). It is inscribed to William Rothenstein ("Dearest Will— | Would this amuse | you? Your affectionate | Max"). Under the text is written: "Th*m*s H*rdy. | M*x Gate, July 20th, 1923." Lord David Cecil, Oxford, has two earlier versions of this poem.

Published in S. N. Behrman, *Conversation with Max* (London, 1960), pp. 83-84; *idem, Portrait of Max* (New York, 1960), pp. 101-102.

Stanza 3, line 2: "antient": archaic spelling of "ancient."

§ 70. *Tracked*

The Winter Owl, edited by Robert Graves and William Nicholson (London, Cecil Palmer, 1923), p. 20. Printed from the copy in the Libraries of the University of Buffalo, by courtesy of Professor Robert Graves, Deyá, Mallorca, Spain, and Mr. David Posner, Lockwood Memorial Library, Buffalo, New York. Mr. William A. von Metz, Oakland, California, has a slightly different version, titled "Night-Piece."

Cf. Beerbohm's "Enoch Soames" in *Seven Men* (London, 1919), pp. 1-48; *see also* Nos. 35 and 36.

Line 11: Radziwill: probably an imaginary character.

§ 71. *In Max's copy of Ianthe Dunbar's* The Edge of the Desert

Sotheby's *Catalogue*, p. 22. Title supplied by editor. *The Edge of the Desert* was published in 1923.

§ 72. *Ballade of an Old Fogey*

From the autograph manuscript in the Harvard College Library (MS Eng

696.16). The Library also possesses an earlier, considerably revised draft of this poem.

Stanza 2, line 7: Augustus Edwin John (1878-1961), British painter.

§ 73. *On Proust*

Alfred Sutro, *Celebrities and Simple Souls* (London, 1933), p. 84. Title supplied by editor.

"On one occasion, when Max had come to town for a short stay, he confessed to not having read Marcel Proust, and my wife insisted on lending him a copy of *Du Côté de Chez Swann,* that Max took away with him. Time passed; months passed; not a word came from Max. The book was a first edition that my wife valued; so she wrote and reminded him. By return came the book, embellished by a drawing of himself as a penitent holding a candle, and a letter: 'Peccavi! The sin that I mean is of course my not having returned the book. But don't ever trust me again! As to my failure to believe in Proust's method, I have put an apology for *that* on the page after the drawing. And here is the apology: [follows text of the poem]."—*Ibid,* pp. 83-84.

Line 6: Charles Kenneth Scott Moncrieff translated a number of books by Marcel Proust into English and edited *Marcel Proust: An English Tribute* (1923).

Lines 8-9: *cf.* Thomas Brown's translation of Martial, *Epigrams,* i, 32 (*Works,* 1719, IV, p. 113):

> I do not love you Dr. Fell,
> But why I cannot tell;
> But this I know full well,
> I do not love you, Dr. Fell.

I have dropped the hyphen in "Scott-Moncrieff" (line 6), and added a comma after line 8.

§ 74. *Sonnet to the 'Most Distinguished Chancellor' that Oxford Has Had*

Autograph manuscript, with revisions and deletions, on Villino Chiaro letterhead, in the William W. Clary Oxford Collection at the Honnold Library of The Claremont Colleges, Claremont, California. Reproduced in facsimile in *A Keepsake to Commemorate the Visit of the Grolier Club of New York and the Zamorano Club of Los Angeles to the William W. Clary Oxford Collection at the Honnold Library of the Associated Colleges,*

Claremont, California, April 28, 1961. Lord David Cecil, Oxford, has a slightly different text.

The sonnet is a parody of Wordsworth's "London, 1802":

> Milton ! thou shouldst be living at this hour:
> England hath need of thee: she is a fen
> Of stagnant waters: altar, sword, and pen,
> Fireside, the heroic wealth of hall and bower,
> Have forfeited their ancient English dower
> Of inward happiness. We are selfish men;
> Oh ! raise us up, return to us again;
> And give us manners, virtue, freedom, power.
> Thy soul was like a Star, and dwelt apart;
> Thou hadst a voice whose sound was like the sea:
> Pure as the naked heavens, majestic, free,
> So didst thou travel on life's common way,
> In cheerful godliness; and yet thy heart
> The lowliest duties on herself did lay.

Max sent his parody to Harold Nicolson shortly after Lord Cave had defeated Asquith in the election for the Chancellorship of Oxford University in 1925.

Line 1: George Nathaniel Curzon, first Marquis Curzon of Kedleston, Chancellor of Oxford University, 1907-1925.

Line 2: Harold George Nicolson, author of *Curzon: The Last Phase. A Study in Post-War Diplomacy* (1934); George Cave, Viscount Cave, Chancellor of Oxford University, 1925-1928.

Line 6: Arthur Wellesley, first Duke of Wellington, Chancellor of Oxford University, 1834-1852.

Line 8: Robert Arthur Talbot Gascoyne-Cecil, third Marquis of Salisbury, Chancellor of Oxford University, 1869-1903.

Line 11: *cf.* George Meredith, *The Egoist* (The World's Classics), Ch. II, p. 11: "Mrs. Mountstuart touched a thrilling chord. 'In spite of men's hateful modern costume, you see he has a leg.' That is, the leg of the born cavalier is before you . . . And the ladies knew for a fact that Willoughby's leg was exquisite."

§ 75. *On Sir Alfred Mond*

Autograph manuscript, signed "M. B.," owned by Mr. Rupert Hart-Davis, London. Title supplied by editor.

The epigram was inspired by the following paragraph of a letter from Sir Alfred Mond to the Editor of *The Times*, 6 March 1926: "If clearing the air and expressing the opinion of thousands of plain people is disastrous, then the epithet may be deserved."

Alfred Moritz Mond, first Baron Melchett (1868-1930), industrialist, financier, and politican.

§ 76. *In the Store-Room at King's Land*

Facsimile reproduction in Sotheby's *Catalogue*, p. 15. Written by Max on the flyleaf of his presentation copy of Hilaire Belloc's *Belinda* (1928). Dated "New Year, 1929" and signed "M. B. | to | H. B." The same lines, in Max's autograph, occur on the half-title of his presentation copy of Belloc's *Sonnets and Verse* (1923); on the opposite page there is the following autograph pencil note: "I sent these lines to him after Florence and I had lunched at his house, in the dawn of 1929. M. B."—*Cf.* Sotheby's *Catalogue*, Nos. 32, 34, 291.

Reprinted, with minor variants, and accompanied by a letter from Sir Max Beerbohm, in *The Sunday Times*, 23 July 1950, p. 3 ("80th Birthday Tributes to Hilaire Belloc").

Hilaire Belloc lived at King's Land, Shipley, Horsham, Surrey.

§ 77. *Epitaph for G. B. Shaw*

Communicated by Professor Craig LaDrière through Professor G. Giovannini, Washington, D. C.

The source of this "epitaph" is Ezra Pound, who recited it to Professor Giovannini from memory at least twice while he was an inmate at St. Elizabeth's Hospital in Washington (1945-1958). Later, after his release, Pound repeated the lines in the company of Professor Giovannini's friend and colleague Craig LaDrière, who recorded them with Pound's permission.

Professor LaDrière questions the word "epitaph" in the title; but Professor Giovannini remembers that it is the title Pound gave to the verse when he first recited it to him: "Maxie's epitaph . . ."

Pound lived at Rapallo from around 1924 until 1945.

§ 78. *The Road to Zoagli*

Autograph manuscript owned by Mr. E. E. Bissell, Ashorne, Warwick. The poem, which is written on Villino Chiaro letterhead, bears the inscription: "For Florence Hardy, | with affectionate regards, | this thing that amused | her. | Max Beerbohm | 1930," and is illustrated with a sketch of a cloaked figure with the legend "The w-b-n-h-d | was of this kind." It is preserved in a folder with a paper label "From the Library of Thomas Hardy, O.M. Max Gate," and has "Lot 296" in blue pencil on the front.

Cecil James Sharp (1859-1924), arranger of English folk songs and dances.

§ 79. *After Kipling's 'Recessional'*

This parody was added by Max to the frontispiece, captioned "The house of 'The Light that Failed'," in his copy of Frederic Whyte's *A Bachelor's London* (1931). The frontispiece, which also contains a caricature portrait of Kipling by Max, is reproduced in Sotheby's *Catalogue*, illustrated edition, plate facing p. 67.

Title supplied by editor.

§ 80. *To the Editor of* The Isis

Reply to an invitation to contribute something for Eights' Week Number of *The Isis* (Oxford), May 1932. Typescript in the Beerbohm Collection, Library of Merton College, Oxford (Provisional Catalogue No. 7.15).

§ 81. *Addition to Kipling's 'The Dead King (Edward VII.), 1910'*

Autograph manuscript owned by Mr. Jay Hall, Statesville, North Carolina. The stanza is written at the bottom of p. 222 of Rudyard Kipling's *Verse, 1885-1932* (London, 1933). Title supplied by editor.

§ 82. *Old Surrey Saws and Sayings*

The Abinger Chronicle, vol. I, No. 5 (April 1940), p. 42. The autograph manuscript was purchased by Francis Edwards Ltd, London, at the Sotheby sale in 1960 of Beerbohm's library and literary mss.

The *Chronicle* was a little venture during World War II, which kept Max, Robert Trevelyan, E. M. Forster and other local luminaries occupied on at least a few of the more dreary wartime evenings. Max wrote a few essays and drew for the little magazine.

Abinger Hammer is a village two miles from Abinger Common. The Abinger Hatch is the inn opposite Abinger Common Church. Both are commonly referred to, in the district, as the "Hammer" and the "Hatch." Bookham, Stonebridge and Dorking are towns on the way to London. Dorking (28,000 inhabitants) is the nearest town to Abinger Common, being 4½ miles away. Sir Max and Lady Beerbohm lived at Abinger Manor Cottage during the war. (Information communicated by Sylvia Sprigge, Editor of *The Abinger Chronicle*, Cherry Cottage, Abinger Common, Surrey.)

§ 83. *February 14th 1945*

Communicated by Lord David Cecil, Oxford.

§ 84. *To Dr. D.*

Written for Oliver Brown in 1952 when Max was eighty years old, and is the only discoverable verse composed from the time of his return to Rapallo in 1947 until his death in 1956.

Mr. Brown was the representative of the Leicester Galleries with whom he dealt when writing about arrangements for exhibitions. The Galleries celebrated his eightieth anniversary with a show of his caricatures, *"Max" in Retrospect*, in May 1952.

Line 1: "Doctor Dryasdust": Dr. Jonas Dryasdust, an imaginary clergyman, prolix and learned, to whom Walter Scott addressed the prefaces to certain of his novels.

Line 4: Sir Herbert Edward Read (b. 1893), British poet and critic, whose *The Philosophy of Modern Art* (London, 1952) could have inspired this reaction to his prose style.

INDEX of TITLES
and FIRST LINES

First lines of poems are in full italics, titles are indicated by roman type.

INDEX OF PERSONS

The references are to pages